FIREPLACES
for a beautiful home

Beautiful Homes Series

First edition for the United States and Canada published 1990 by Barron's Educational Series, Inc.

© Text Copyright 1989 by Katherine Seppings
© Copyright 1989 by Merehurst Limited
By arrangement with Dunestyle Publishing Ltd.

First published in Great Britain in 1989 by Merehurst Press, London, England

All inquiries should be addressed to:
Barron's Educational Series, Inc.
250 Wireless Boulevard
Hauppauge, New York 11788

Library of Congress Catalog Card No. 89-2716
International Standard Book No. 0-8120-6170-5
Library of Congress Cataloging-in-Publication Data

Seppings, Katherine.
    Fireplaces for a beautiful home/Katherine Seppings.
    — 1st ed.
    160 p.
    ISBN 0-8120-6170-5
    1. Fireplaces.   I. Title.
TH7425.S46   1990
721'.8—dc20   89-27168
                                                   CIP

Printed in Italy by New Interlitho s.p.a., Milan

0123   987654321

Half-title page A simple Victorian-style fireplace with a gleaming brass fender and accessories.

Title page An Adam-style fireplace decorated with fluting, swags and an urn.

Contents page A classical-style pine surround featuring roundels and fluting, with a reproduction Victorian cast-iron inset.

FIREPLACES
for a beautiful home

Katherine Seppings

Katherine Seppings

BARRON'S

NEW YORK · TORONTO

CONTENTS

Right This polished cast-iron reproduction fireplace, Peace and Plenty, depicts theatrical motifs in the style of the seventeenth century architect, Inigo Jones.

Above Fruit, flowers, and the statue of Plenty, executed in high relief, provided elegant touches to a grand fireplace.

The history of the fireplace is not only an architectural and interior design story; it provides a central clue to the maze of mystery and myths that have traditionally drawn us to the warm and comforting hearth. Although we are no longer dependent on fire in its purest form, in the intimacy of our homes we continue to defy the stormy weather and bitter cold by the fireside. The play of dancing flames, the glow of coals, the crackling and gentle roar awaken memories and instincts, warming our bodies and soothing our restless minds. The love and fear of fire is inherent in all of us, lying deep within our universal unconscious. From the earliest spark kindled, everyone, no matter how rich or poor, has desired and needed fire, has been mesmerized by its magic and lured by its majesty.

Its discovery in the Stone Age gave human beings a domestic hearth as a means of heating, cooking, and illumination. Being able to control fire enabled an advancement in the production of stone-made tools and allowed primitive people the freedom to travel into colder climates. The symbolic nature of fire led the Chinese and Greeks to include it along with earth, air, and water as one of the four basic elements of life. In Greek mythology the hero Prometheus brought fire to earth by stealing it from Zeus, who had destructive plans for the mortals below. It is said that fire then saved our fate. Such legends the world over have meant that it has been feared and revered in religious worship and rituals since its very birth.

The earliest remains of an actual hearth date back some 500,000 years, although hearths have more commonly been found on Paleolithic sites dating back 200,000 years. However, the more recent discovery of fire-hardened clay in Kenya reveals the possibility of a hearth 1.4 million years old. This new

INTRODUCTION

Right Exposed handmade bricks and solid timber beams incorporated into the mantelpiece give true rustic charm to this cottage fireplace.

Above A 'hole-in-the-wall' design is ideal for the simplistic, sparse feel of a modern interior and does not compete with additional decoration. The polished brass trim around the opening complements the brass fire tools and coal bucket. The hearth base has been extended to provide a marble-finished surface for fireplace accessories or additional seating.

evidence could alter the history of the hearth quite dramatically; it may indicate that the human ability to use fire to our advantage was an event that happened far earlier than has previously been thought and originated in Africa, rather than in Europe and Asia.

Fireplaces throughout the world have taken numerous and diverse forms, often serving various functions. The Eskimos mastered a fireplace built within an ice house, the igloo. North American Indians used their fireplaces not only for fundamental warmth but, through smoke signals from their tepees, used the fireplace as a unique system of communication. The tepee had an entrance flap that could be closed at ground level and a sophisticated system of adjustable flaps at the top to regulate heat and smoke flow; the hearth itself was a small, central, stone-lined pit. Tribal life among the Australian Aborigines was similar to that of the North American Indians. The Aborigines practiced "firestick husbandry," the slow burning of small areas of land to manage and capture game. The land was their home, and as they sheltered in caves and rough shanties in the cooler regions, life was centered around the hearth. In the drier, hotter areas, where they had little need even for shanty huts, the hearth was literally the home. In addition, the Aborigines developed an early version of the oven, made from stone.

In early Europe and the British Isles tribal people in their scanty shelters slept on beds of furs, grasses, and leaves placed around an open fire. This type of open hearth hut is still used today in Nepal and the Andes. The hill tribes of Thailand and Burma still burn green kindling on a thick stone slab, positioned in a tripod form so that the timber, lit from the top, burns slowly in a downward direction. The people of Kashmir continue to cart their fireplaces around

with them in the form of charcoal-filled firepots carried beneath the "farren," a loose-fitting heavy woolen smock.

Nowadays, however, it is important to remember that with the reduction in the amount of available timber throughout the world, fireplaces have been modified to become more heat efficient, as well as changing their appearance to satisfy the dreams of artistic designers.

Today, only eight percent of Britain's 57 million acres of land is covered by forests. North America's once vast reserves have been ravaged and South America's rain forests are diminishing rapidly. Not all the world's precious timber has "gone up in smoke," but over the past few centuries we have been forced to use alternative fuels, such as coal, oil, gas, and electricity, because of the indulgence of

previous societies when trees were plentiful. As each decade passes fewer homes will be able to display the welcoming stack of logs, stored for the cold winter months; for the millions of people living in high-density cities this is already history.

In spite of our concern with the disappearance of the forests, fireplaces bring to everyone not only a feeling of warmth and relaxation but, by appealing to all our senses, a feeling of being down to earth — a part of nature. Fireplaces have remained in our hearts as we refuse to succumb to this modern age of push-button convenience. Although supplanted by central heating in the last few decades, the open fire has been a consistent architectural feature of homes in Britain, North America, and Australia. History does repeat itself; the fireplace is once again the heart of the home.

CHAPTER 1

Right Since the Middle Ages inglenooks, with their large timber beams and deep recess, have provided the family with warmth and cosiness. Here, this warm climate family of cats can appreciate the heat, radiated with the aid of a decorative fireback.

Above One of the major attractions of cast-iron stoves is their ability to fit into almost any type of existing fireplace. The glass doors provide the visual focus of an open fire, with the efficiency and economy of a closed stove.

The origin of the fireplace as we know it today was devised by the Norman military engineer-architects for the palatial stone castles being built all over England. The central hearth fire was not practical in these multistoried fortresses, so the wall fireplace was designed and built as an integral part of the stone wall structure.

In more humble homes the central hearth survived. Around the central fireplace lay dry rushes or straw, strewn over the floor, to keep the dampness at bay. Exposed timbers ignited easily in these conditions. It may have been for this reason that the curfew was introduced in 1068. The church bell was tolled at 8 o'clock every evening, warning people to retreat to their homes and cover their fires. The word curfew comes from the French *couvre feu*, which literally means "cover fire" and was also the name given to a metal cover put down over the fire to reduce the risk of escaping embers while retaining the hot coals ready for the next morning. It is also said that the curfew was introduced to restrict people from socializing in the evenings, those in power being fearful of rebellion.

In early days, the servants joined their lords for supper and then slept around the fire, and the noble family and guests occupied the raised dais above.

Central Hearth Versus Wall Fireplace

Life in Britain in medieval times was short, harsh, and even barbaric. It was a society largely based on a strict feudal system, a well-defined class structure within close communal living and dominated by the Church. The nobility with their retinue of servants were, to a degree, nomadic, continually moving about to oversee their huge estates and protect their territories. Their castles and manor houses were heavily fortified and usually moated. Since they feared barbarian invasions so much, they were far

more concerned with security than with interior decoration or comfort. Their homes appeared as bleak as the winter climate and, whether humble homes or palaces, were hall-shaped structures.

The development of the fireplace became as varied as the wealth of the people. The majority of people continued to stoke the central hearth, as it was cheap to build, more heat efficient, and allowed the tradition of homeliness, where family and friends would gather around the fire that sustained them. The central hearth fireplace served as a heating and cooking system. Iron firedogs, or andirons, were positioned in front of the hearth so that meat could be spit-roasted. These were replaced in the fourteenth century by lateral firedogs, used to support logs on the fire.

Only the wealthy upper level of society could afford to adopt the Norman wall fireplace, as it required skilled craftsmen and expensive materials. By the midtwelfth century the changing economy and social ideas were reflected in the new interest directed toward arts and literature. Chivalry, lavish ceremonies, and entertainment became the accepted way of life for those of the court. Christian art reflected these changing social attitudes, and the heavy Norman architecture made way for the uplifting, lighter, and more orderly Gothic style. During this period many grand monasteries were built, most of which had wall fireplaces displaying fine designs and craftsmanship. In fact, the Gothic fireplace had developed from a shallow recess in the wall with a flue into a platform, above which extended a pyramidal hood. In the course of the fifteenth century the entire fireplace was recessed, the chimney piece and surround being one, flush against the wall with a Gothic arch at the opening.

By this time privacy, comfort, and decoration were given serious attention. Privacy was still only available to those who held positions of great importance; comfort and decoration followed closely behind. It is thought that the first complete wall fireplaces were actually built in the sleeping chamber, which soon became a highly decorated room.

The Cultural Separation

In the Middle Ages, the fireplace held a prominent position as the focus for family life, the

Left This massive fireplace with hand-carved red gum timbers was built in a mudbrick barn at Montsalvat in Melbourne, Victoria, Australia during World War II, as part of the war effort. It was later turned into an artist's studio and retains an earthy feel with its warm slate floor and other local materials.

heart of social intimacy, radiating warmth for fundamental needs and inspiring myths and legends.

The idea had been kindled in the minds of cold climate people to view the fireplace as a central decorative piece of architecture, but it was not until the upheaval of the Reformation and the Renaissance that the hearth ranked as the most important interior feature in this new era of arts and architecture.

During the reign of Henry VIII enormous changes took place in Britain. Cutting ties with the Roman Catholic Church meant, to a certain extent, the isolation of British art and architecture from European cultural influence. Nevertheless, it did force new ideas to emerge throughout the Tudor, Elizabethan, and Jacobean periods. The sixteenth century has been criticized by many as a time when English architecture was given poor patronage by the monarchy, and interiors seemed gloomy, ill conceived, and lacking unity in their designs. In the early sixteenth century Italian homes were said to be the envy of Europe, and at this period Britain did remain, on the whole, isolated from the heart of the Italian Renaissance.

Many old traditions became shaken or even foresaken. A major consideration by the late sixteenth century was the scarcity of timber as a building material. During the Elizabethan period much timber was used in shipbuilding. As a source of fuel timber was even more scarce, and such alternatives as coal were looming as a possibility.

During this age of development and social reform, such internal structures as the ceiling were added to the traditional hall house, to conserve heat and to create a second story. The use of brick in building became more popular, and hence brick chimneys appeared too.

Above Exterior fireplace.

Below Sixteenth century English inglenook at Oakhurst Cottage. Large solid lintels or slabs of marble were often decorated with the marks of the adze, carved armorial bearings, or Tudor roses and foliage.

The problem of where to place the fireplace was dealt with in various ways. Some cottages were serviced by a single central fireplace with chimney, but as rooms were added additional fireplaces were built against the exterior wall. It was this fashion for building on rooms that eventually meant the end of the central fireplace, for the majority of people began to favor the wall fireplace, despite the loss of much heat up the chimney and the reduced social interaction it fostered from its position. An alternative arrangement that maintained and encouraged cosiness was the great, deep fireplace or inglenook that was found in small cottages and wealthier homes alike. For the less well-off the rooms were usually quite small and simple in their design, incorporating large timber beams constructed, as they were in medieval times, with functional purposes in mind.

Oak, which had once been used abundantly, was now restricted to more refined features, such as

Below Free-standing convector fireboxes are highly suitable for inglenooks, as they direct the heat forward from the deep recess. A neat stack of logs ready to throw on the fire always adds a welcoming sight to the hearth.

carved wall panels and beams. Large, solid lintels or mantels were decorated with the marks of the adze, carved armorial bearings, or Tudor roses or foliage, often delicately painted with gentle shades of red, ocher, and green. Stone Tudor arches were used where afforded, the grandest style having four arches at the opening to the fireplace.

We can still appreciate the appeal of the inglenook, which could accommodate utensils for cooking, drying clothes, and smoking bacon and space for a hungry family. Inglenooks provided the family with a cosy cooking facility, incorporating spits and cloam ovens. In early times spits were turned by small children and even dogs, but later weight pulleys were used. Cloam ovens, built of brick and clay, were built into the side of the inglenook fireplace, higher up the wall with a stone floor and dome-shaped roof. The opening was sealed with a large stone. The idea of these ovens originated in the Stone Age, when they were used outdoors; many early tribes raked out the hot embers and used the oven's absorbed heat as a means of baking bread. The oven evolved by fitting cast-iron doors. Early examples can still be found in Scotland, Wales, and Cornwall; and Colonial Dutch ovens of similar design can still be found in New York State.

Many changes occurred in this century's consciousness. A new interest in forestry conservation emerged, together with an awareness of fire safety requirements in the home. Before the sixteenth century smoke hoods, often built of wattle and daub, were a fire risk, as were the modest hearths built against timber interior room-partitioned walls. In London, building laws were introduced to ensure that chimneys were built only of brick or stone, with surrounding materials being noncombustible tiles or plaster. These strict controls were probably another reason for the disappearance of the central hearth fireplace.

Henry VIII and Cardinal Wolsey imported Italian craftsmen to adorn lavish and important fireplaces, but generally Renaissance aesthetic ideals did not reach Britain easily. This creative isolation resulted in the sixteenth century fireplace developing as a unique and special decorative composition, yet lacking the grace and elegance of the splendid

European designs. Fireplaces were not treated as part of the structure as a whole. Many were imported from Italy, Spain, Portugal, and France. In Britain early-Renaissance decoration was overdone and seemed out of place; equally, the Gothic ornamentation of the previous centuries did not make for unity in the overall design of a room. During this transition period between the two styles

Below Henry VIII imported Italian craftsmen to adorn lavish and important fireplaces, such as the one at Reigate Priory, from Nonsuch Palace. The detail shows how the classical Renaissance combined with a medieval style resulted in a unique decorative composition.

there was no fixed style. Although some fireplaces were built to a definite fashion, the majority were functional and solid and were not designed to be particularly decorative. Indeed, it was not until the later part of the sixteenth century that the Renaissance was felt in Britain and medieval designs were finally superseded.

The theatrical mood of Elizabethan and Jacobean times was reflected in important buildings. A room or great hall became a stage on which designers featured the fireplace, magnificent in all its roaring glory. Designers sought inspiration from Flemish and German ornamental pattern books. Strapwork, an intricate geometric decoration, emerged from this source and became a feature of late Elizabethan and Jacobean decoration.

Britain remained isolated from the dramatic influence of the Italian Renaissance. However, ornamental details included Italianate elements, combining interlacing strapwork with carved diamond patterns, ovals, shields, coats of arms, and floral emblems. Heraldic or scriptural subjects were commonly displayed, carved in stone, brick, or oak. Delicate classical figures were mixed with graceful Gothic foliage, combining Renaissance and medieval styles.

The Influence of Architects

The lack of harmony in sixteenth century interiors was resolved in the seventeenth century through a new concept of rules and expertise. Italianate design, which had not been easily accommodated into sixteenth century British architecture and interior design, became more established in the seventeenth century.

This new age of objective inquiry and humanism, incorporating the study of mathematics and philosophy, was first seen in literature, followed by

Left The early sixteenth century
fireplace emerged as a central
decorative piece of architecture.
It was often criticized as lacking unity
in its design, especially when
compared with examples that were
clearly influenced by the Italian
Renaissance. Despite severing
cultural ties with Europe, Henry VIII
ensured that his own fireplace at
Nonsuch Palace, now at Reigate
Priory, followed the Italian fashion.

the visual arts and then architecture. This cultural awakening resulted in the traditional Gothic and English Perpendicular styles merging with a new classical style. In many cases the traditional decorative styles were not lost, and a hybrid classical style resulted. The flourishing artistic ideas of the seventeenth century meant the gradual diminishing of haphazard craftsmanship and design. Less imaginative styles, which had evolved because they suited available materials and resources and were not, therefore, governed by any prevailing conception of decorative intent, began to disappear.

The most notable revolution of this century directly related to the subject of fireplaces was the emergence of the first trained architects, professionals who were entirely responsible for design and construction. Individual architects did not have an immediate effect on the majority of homes. New and important buildings required their services, but further down the scale of wealth the influence was diminished. As with any new idea or fashion, it takes time to reach the majority of

Below and right This midseventeenth century fireplace, blended into an oak-paneled room, depicts Adam and Eve in the carved overmantel. At a time when classical architecture and design were flourishing in Europe, medieval designs were still gracefully displayed in the warm wood and cool stone surrounds in Britain.

people, and in the seventeenth century it took up to fifty years before the assimilation took place.

The wall fireplace provided the perfect facade for the upper class to display their wealth and status in society. The great Jacobean fireplaces were excellent examples of elaborate decoration incorporating the owner's coat of arms or symbols of his profession. Jacobean interiors were heavily influenced by European, particularly Dutch, designers. The source of their decorative detail can in many cases be traced to Dietterlin's *Architectura*, published at the end of the sixteenth century.

Inigo Jones

The real change in fireplace design and decoration came with the first professional architects adhering to the strict rules of Vitruvius in *De Architectura* and Palladio in his *Quattro Libri*. The first architect to introduce the purest Renaissance ideas and initiate English classical architecture was Inigo Jones and, following him, his pupil, John Webb. Inigo Jones became chief architect to the crown in 1615. He was the first architect and interior designer to have any true understanding of classical dignity. In addition, he was able to unite the form, composition, and proportion of the fireplace within the whole dimensions of the interior. He believed above all in a basic functional fireplace design, and from there on added decoration, although never at the expense of the underlying design.

One of the best surviving seventeenth century English interiors, the Double Cube Room at Wilton House, Wiltshire, England, is a memorable example of the work Inigo Jones produced. The exquisite fireplace is one of the first ever created in white marble and gilded timber to match the walls of the room. The marble was carved in Italy,

displaying beautiful swags, fluted columns, drapery weaving in and out, inlaid colored marble, crests, scrolls, statues of Peace and Plenty, reclining figures, busts, and magnificent pediments. The overall effect is theatrical but elegant. Fruit, flowers, and palms, executed in high relief and gilded, are a constant theme of ornament, continuing around the large panels and boldly outlined by moldings. Paintings, including the inset picture by Van Dyke above the fireplace, were incorporated as part of the design.

Although there were other architects at the time of Inigo Jones, they all consulted one another, relying heavily on each other's ideas, tending to produce work in a similar vein and lacking Jones' originality. Decoration was left to the craftsmen who invariably used the same standardized patterns. The lack of originality among many craftsmen at this period explains why many baroque marble chimneypieces were also being imported from Italy, or made by Italian craftsmen.

By the time of Inigo Jones' death in 1652, the British version of classical architecture and design was flourishing and a highly civilized age had begun.

Christopher Wren

Christopher Wren was the next great architect and became Inigo Jones' successor as Chief Architect to the Crown. Although Wren did not design many domestic interiors, he was responsible for introducing a quite different style. Following the Great Fire of London, in 1666, Wren took up the task of rebuilding St. Paul's Cathedral, along with fifty other churches destroyed in the fire. The Great Fire had a tremendous impact upon the architectural face of London, with so many thousands of old timber buildings gone forever.

During the second half of the seventeenth century the standard of craftmanship had advanced toward matching that of the highly skilled European craftsmen. Wren was fortunate enough to call on the expertise of such men as Grinling Gibbons, who became known as the greatest of all wood carvers, with his naturalistic style.

Peculiar to Wren's designs was the treatment of the surrounding area to the fireplace opening. This surround was simply framed with heavy relief molding in stone or marble. The overmantel was now conceived as a part of the wall paneling. Mirrors were frequently incorporated within the overmantel, with shelves to display fashionable delftware or other special china pieces. In Europe, overmantel mirrors appeared early in the century, but it was not until the end of the seventeenth century that they became widespread in Britain. In the Netherlands it was far more popular to hang oil paintings above the mantel and on all available wall space. Here, the fireplace still dominated the room with its strong vertical and horizontal classical lines.

In England the overmantel was adorned with beautiful oak carving by Grinling Gibbons, who was commissioned to leave his mark on most wealthy homes at this time. He had the ability to sculpture fantasies of nature with impeccable fineness. His superb decorations were usually representations of birds, flowers, fruit, and, in some cases, sheaves of wheat, fish, and coats of arms. Many carvings of that era said to be the work of Gibbons may have been executed by his imitators, although there is no doubt that he was a prolific craftsman. However, a fireplace adorned with his genuine carvings can be recognized by his own mark: an open pea pod.

Another notable feature of Wren's designs was the corner fireplace, a fashion he adopted from France. This style was a clear sign of the artificiality

Below Detail of a classical scene from a fireplace overmantel at the Marble Hall, Clanden Park, Surrey, England. The fireplace was designed by Rysbrack.

Right Mantelpieces and overmantels, such as this example at the Marble Hall, Clandon Park, Surrey, followed the strict classical principles of Palladio. Scaled-down versions of this period would have incorporated columns and scrolls in their decoration.

Below Eighteenth century Palladian interiors were designed as a whole. Marble Hall was designed by Leoni, who advocated the serious approach to architecture and achieved perfect symmetrical balance.

of the age and of the times to come. The fireplace, traditionally the focus of the home and family life, was now relegated to a corner, making it virtually impossible for people to gather around its warmth. It also made arranging furniture more difficult, so the corner fireplace was most often found in bedrooms, where fireplaces in general were becoming far more common. During this period there was a fashionable preference for large windows, and heat conservation must have presented its problems.

Early Georgian

The splendor of the baroque, the ornate intimacy of rococo, the seriousness of the Palladian style, the genius of Adam, and the revolutions of Rumford all mark the unsurpassed richness and quality of eighteenth century fireplaces.

The baroque style of fireplaces, which began to appear in the late seventeenth century, did not lend itself to scaled-down versions for smaller homes; it was a grand style for the elite. People with large homes could afford large marble mantelpieces and elaborate wood overmantels with a baroque painting built into a central panel.

Many pattern books and works of great architects were published and builders of the time adapted numerous designs. On the whole, however, early Georgian fireplaces were often very plain structures. These simple examples are expensive today because of their rarity. By 1720, architects began to reject the baroque style in favor of Palladio's designs, which could be simplified and were therefore far more appropriate to the majority of interiors.

In Europe another style emerged: the light, fresh rococo, which, although rejected by British architects, became characteristic of French and German town houses. Opposing strict Palladian rules of symmetry, the fireplace opening was fitted with strips of marble, curved with a line of beauty. The elongated S shapes were called serpentine lines and were used wherever possible.

The most popular material for the surround was colored marble, especially *marbre d'Antin*, a rich mixture of red, yellow, and violet, streaked with gray. Oval mirrors in the overmantel were very popular, and in some homes the use of mirrors was extravagant: entire walls and ceilings and, during the summer, even fireplace openings were lined with mirrors. Chimneypieces were often decorated with gilded bronze, known as ormolu, on carved wood or molded plaster. Such motifs as delicate flowers, foliage, and ribbons were used abundantly,

Left The elaborate fireplace in the Green Drawing Room, Clandon Park, Surrey, is decorated with ormolu, gilded bronze on carved wood or molded plaster. The classical painting set into the overmantel reflects the green hues of the 1735 wallpaper.

Far left Classical white marble fireplaces are characteristic of eighteenth century interiors. The delicate swags on the mantelpiece in the Palladio Room at Clandon Park, Surrey, are typical of the simplified decoration.

Below A treatment known as Bossi work, which involved carving out white marble and then filling it with decorative colored marble, was popularized in the late Georgian period. This detail of the Hatchlands dining room mantelpiece shows a molding reminiscent of the Greek *echinus* pattern surrounding an ornate version of fluting.

Right The soft yellow and pale green in the dining room of Hatchlands, Surrey, is reflected in the large overmantel mirror and emphasized by the gold-painted delicate moldings. The warmer colors blended with the pale pastels convey a lighter, more playful feel.

Far right Instead of placing individual emphasis on the fireplace, Robert Adam's decorative schemes included colors that linked the chimneypiece to other features. Here, the library fireplace at Hatchlands, by Adam, includes his typical round medallions and bas reliefs of classical figures.

and ornate candelabra were a common feature.

Evidence of the influence that the rococo period had on Britain can be found in the *gothick* style. This was more of a fantasy style than an accurate copy of medieval ornament. Horace Walpole became famous for his *gothick* fireplace designs, many of his ideas coming from tombs in Westminster Abbey and reflecting their "monumental" quality. A number of sculptors worked on both marble chimneypieces and monuments for the church, bringing about an interesting interplay of design ideas. William Kent (1684–1778), who was known for reviving Palladian themes, occasionally adopted a *gothick* style. Under Robert Adam's influence, Walpole improved some of his designs by introducing scagliola, inlaid in white marble. Scagliola is an artificially formed marble, made up of powdered marble, lime, gypsum, and sometimes plaster, glued together and then polished. Apart from being warmer to the touch than marble, it was often a very good imitation and became fashionable in its own right.

Kent had a solid knowledge of Palladian architecture but drew heavily on Jones' style for his own fireplace designs. It was his strong belief in designing the interior as a whole that led to the characteristic and classical white marble fireplace of the eighteenth century.

Palladian designs were revived after 1715, and the exotic fashions for baroque, *gothick*, and chinoiserie began to disappear in favor of a more formal style. Neoclassicism signaled a dignified and serious approach to architecture. However, Kent's designs, although simple, were always scaled to large buildings and were not meant for small homes.

Following strict classical principles, Palladian fireplaces decorated with columns and scrolls were suitable for formal rooms. In smaller homes the

Below This striking fireplace at Hatchlands, with its dominant Greek *key* pattern and Italian Bossi work, has an air of stately importance.

drawing room was paneled in pine and displayed a pine mantelpiece, with a marble or stone slip surrounding the opening. All wood was painted, unless it was oak, which it rarely was as pine was the most commonly used timber. In large homes mantelpieces were generally of marble and walls were plastered or decorated with wallpaper, often with Chinese-style designs. Distinctively Palladian architectural features were most apparent on the exteriors of homes; to achieve symmetrical balance, chimneys were built at the gable ends. Stacks were frequently placed on the adjoining walls between the terraced houses and were constructed as low as possible, so as not to interfere with the skyline.

Left "In the beautiful spirit of antiquity," Adam substituted standard decoration with beautiful classical figures in a style used by the Romans themselves to ornament their palaces and baths. The deep red of the wall panels, echoed in the Persian rug, adds to the opulence of this room at Hatchlands, Surrey.

Far left Adam made a feature of using such ornament as small paintings, medallions, urns, busts, and candelabra. The variety of light moldings in the sitting room at Hatchlands is typical of Adam's interiors.

Late Georgian

Today when we think of eighteenth century fireplaces, we think of the Adams. Of the Adam brothers the most famous was Robert (1728–92), a unique designer who is ranked as one of the finest decorators of any period or nation. His style dominated British architecture for three decades.

Robert Adam, after studying in Italy from 1754 to 1758, returned to England with new ideas derived from the excavations of Herculaneum, a city buried in 79 A.D. Original Roman decoration was the source of Adam's ornament, and the main feature of his style was the creation of unified, harmonious, and balanced interiors. Adam opposed the bold heaviness of Palladian interiors and fireplaces and

found a new freedom in a lighter classical style.

The typical Adam interior of the 1770s was injected with color, space, and playfulness. Although the backbone of Palladian ideas continued to survive, Adam substituted the standard decoration with "a beautiful variety of light moldings, gracefully formed, delicately enriched, and arranged with propriety and skill . . . in the beautiful spirit of antiquity." Instead of placing individual emphasis on the fireplace, Adam's decorative schemes employed a range of colors in an interior, linking the chimneypiece to other features and using such ornament as small paintings, medallions, scrolls, and swags. The variety of color — pale green, blue, pink, yellow,

Below The hob grate of the eighteenth century still in use two centuries later.

Right The hob grate was set into the entire fireplace opening, one third being the actual grate and on either side metal plates providing an area to heat food and boil a kettle.

and occasionally deep red — was echoed on the doors and the walls, where painted panels were linked by swags, the skirting boards, and chimneypieces. This use of color in fireplace designs had never before been explored to such a degree. His renowned decorative work consisted of low-relief trails and scrolls in bat wing or spider web patterns, oval or round medallions with bas reliefs of classical figures, *anthemion* leaves, and slender swags. Adam called his decorative features grotesque, the name given to the beautiful, light style used by the Romans in the ornament of their palaces, baths, and villas. The ornament was carved in wood, molded in plaster, or rendered in gesso.

Many marble fireplaces in the late Georgian period were decorated with inlaid colored marble. Others were built from or decorated with scagliola. Bartoli, an Italian craftsman, was a master of this material, and Robert Adam used his skills on a number of fireplaces. The method he used, known as "Bossi work," involved carving out white marble and then filling it with decorative colored marble.

In the late 1770s, Josiah Wedgwood began to produce delicate ceramic cameos made from basalt and jasper and set in marble and wood fireplace surrounds. These plaques were usually displayed in contrasting colors of blue or green and white. Eleanor Coade invented an imitation stone from a ceramic composition and produced a variety of decorative ornaments for fireplaces. For the simple dwelling, however, the fireplace was not affected by any of these decorative innovations and was plainly dressed with slabs of stone or slate, the mantel being a separate piece of slate or wood.

The Adam brothers were also involved with the practical requirements of the fireplace. The Coalbrookdale or Carron Company, of which John Adam was a partner, manufactured cast-iron

Below Original Victorian hob grate set into a simple yet lively pine surround.

surrounds, grates, fenders, and fire irons. They all displayed neoclassical motifs and elegant curves. Firedogs and dog grates were still used in fireplaces that burned wood, although hob grates for burning coal became very common in the late eighteenth century. The hob grate was set into the entire fireplace opening, one-third being the actual grate and on either side metal plates or hobs providing an area to heat food and boil a kettle.

CHAPTER 2

Above One of the most popular 1880 designs in marble mantelpieces, cast-iron inserts and cast-iron fenders. The dark gray marble brings a somber note to the morning room.

Right This Victorian burnished steel fireplace was the latest fashion of its time in the 1880s. Styles were incongruous; here this is evident in the combination of line and curve, gold, marble, and steel, classical design with light touches of French styles.

During the twentieth century, with the invention of central heating and the television, the fireplace as the focal point of home living was almost lost forever. The recent revival of concern for the past, however, combined with the traditional fascination with fire , have created a new interest in the fireplace. Today, most people live in houses designed and built in the nineteenth and twentieth centuries. It is these two centuries that this chapter explores to convey a better idea of the original purpose, design, and decorative detailing of each period fireplace. To restore the character and charm of any period house successfully, the restorer must be discriminating and caring. The fireplace should reflect the style in which the house was built. However, many contemporary designs can look good in older settings, too. It is hoped that an overall balance is achieved between understanding and respecting the original features of the house, incorporating an efficient heating system, and displaying one's own personal style.

In discovering the myriad ideas from Victorian and Edwardian times right up to contemporary styles, you will find an array of adaptable designs. This chapter is for your inspiration and deals with period details across two centuries.

The Nineteenth Century

The nineteenth century was the age of the Industrial Revolution. The huge population expansion that occurred during this period led to an unprecedented bout of building. In addition, the period witnessed an enormous interest in interior decoration.

The rising industrial middle classes copied design ideas that would previously have been available only to the most wealthy. Every house equipped

Right A burnished cast-iron fireplace reproduced from an original late-Victorian design. Tiles are used to soften the striking effect of the surround.

itself with mass-produced cast-iron artifacts. All kinds of patented grates and fireplaces were invented and installed, often indiscriminately. Designs similar to those found in wealthy homes became available further down the scale of wealth. Designs were more debased, but more people could benefit in this increasingly mechanized age.

A typical Victorian home had a confusing mishmash of architectural styles, furnishings, and decoration from different periods and, possibly, different cultures. The Victorians were obsessed with ornamental designs. For art historians the Victorian revival of elements derived from earlier periods makes a particularly confusing, although interesting, study.

Nineteenth century eclectism allowed people enormous choice in their interiors. Victorian taste was driven by a romantic nostalgia to re-create the past through careful study of original designs and to stir feelings and evoke moods.

A French architect, Charles Garnier (1825–98), summed up these Victorian sentiments in *Le Style Actuel* (1869): "Each style of architecture has its character, each epoch its beauties . . . everything which is true, everything which is beautiful, must speak to the soul . . . one must be eclectic in order to admire eclecticism."

The Battle of Styles

The battles of styles began prior to the Victorian period, in the early decades of the nineteenth century. For some time to come the basic layout and design of a town house maintained Georgian features, but interior decoration and fireplaces took on all manner of styles.

The popularity of Robert Adam's elegant fireplaces had declined. However, the simplicity of his classicism was revived once more, although the

Below left On a classical surround like this, colorful tile inserts would be quite inappropriate. The controlled lines, fluting, and Adam motifs are best matched with dark marble inserts that compliment the restrained elegance of the fireplace.

Below This burnished cast-iron fireplace is based on an original nineteenth century French design. The Louis XV style favored rococo S shapes and delicate foliage designs. This style continued to be popular throughout the nineteenth century and has been revived recently.

Above A Louis XV style antique French marble mantelpiece, the finely carved frieze decorated with a shell and trails of flowers with acanthus leaves rising from the bases.

term "neoclassicism" was not used until the style became widespread and even international in the 1880s. Within the classical style came a variety of styles, all trying in diverse ways to re-create the feeling of classical Greece and Rome. One of these, the Empire style, in France, was regarded as being "the most chic in domestic decoration" and remained in vogue in Italy when it had all but disappeared in France. Designers were aware of proportion and symmetry, but the neoclassical style lost sight of many of the original principles of design. Fireplaces became much lower in height; the jamb and lintel, made up of plain slabs of smooth marble, became narrower in width; decorations on moldings were minimal, with simple reeding patterns and small corner masks or roundels for ornament. Such was a typical fireplace in a modest English drawing room around 1810.

Depending on the status of the home, the surround was constructed from slate, stone, marble, or timber. The average middle class home gave a feeling of solid respectability. A fireplace similar to that in the drawing room would be found in the dining room. In the dining room, however, Belgian black marble, with the occasional addition of inlaid colored marble panels in the wide jambs, was a popular variation. In rooms of less importance and in the homes of the majority of the population, wood and gesso surrounds or stone surrounds that were either painted or marbleized were used.

White marble fireplaces, with simple Greek Doric columns and a pediment above the frieze, were found only in more wealthy households. Here ornament was restrained and rectangular, often decorated with the Greek *key* pattern. Sir John Soane was an architect famous for this austere style. In his designs he repositioned the frieze over the fireplace opening so that it did not interfere with the

Below When the fireplace was not in use, fire screens were placed in front of the openings and provided yet another area to be decorated.

height of the mantel or prevent the inclusion of an overmantel mirror. Soane preferred the fireplace to act as a base for a large mirror or painting rather than featuring as a composition in itself.

During the nineteenth century plate glass became available. Overmantel mirrors were extremely common, and mahogany was the favorite wood to frame a central mirror, with shelves and smaller mirrors on either side. An interesting concept of building the fireplace beneath the window, common

in the previous century in France, was now experimented with in England. However, the idea did not survive, as seeing the face of a passing stranger in the customary place of one's own reflection over the mantelpiece was too alarming. The overmantel mirror maintained its popularity.

Most fireplaces in France at the beginning of the nineteenth century projected 9 inches (23 cm) from the wall. The front was flat and boxlike with its wide rectangular opening. Today there is a marked

Right The Victorians and Edwardians loved to display bric-a-brac against mahogany, the most favored wood. By the turn of the century decoration had become more sparse. The stylized flowers on the tiles were a typical motif of Art Nouveau design.

increase in the demand for marble fireplaces in this style. For the past twenty years these originals have been exported from France to all parts of the world, but this was not the case in the nineteenth century. Incorporating Louis XV and XVI marble fireplaces where no fireplace existed is a recent trend. They also fit well into a bedroom because they are smaller, although heavier, than English marble fireplaces and are more plentiful. English fireplaces were usually less graceful and stood 58 inches (1.47 m) in height, compared to the 42 to 46 inches (1.05–1.15 m) of French fireplaces. In France they were generally made by Italian craftsmen but were carved and decorated by French craftsmen. Louis XV surrounds and mantels have graceful curves; Louis XVI fireplaces are square and more masculine. The small, feminine Louis XV pompadour has been the most popular fireplace for renovators.

In general, homes began to lose the grace of the Regency period as Victorian taste became established. The harmony of Georgian styles was lost as designers revived neo-Gothic and Elizabethan features. These periods were revived more for what they represented in the nineteenth century than for their architectural elements. For the Victorians the Gothic period symbolized Christian morality and purity. The revived Elizabethan style represented nostalgia for a chivalrous age and also preserved the diminishing status of the nineteenth century gentry.

However, for practical purposes fireplaces had become much smaller, with shallow hearths and tiny firebaskets for coal. The Elizabethan and neoGothic charm was only to be found in the decoration. An array of Gothic, Renaissance, and naturalistic motifs and a theatrical window curtain draped around the overmantel mirror became the

Below A plain classical surround of carved pine can be transformed by introducing a cast-iron inset, decorative and tiled. The fireplace suddenly becomes the focus of the room.

principle elements of these designs.

William Burges was one architect who really revelled in this Middle Ages fantasy world and created brilliantly colored mock medieval chimneypieces. William Beckford, known as England's wealthiest son, commissioned the architect James Wyatt to build Fonthill Abbey in Wiltshire, England (1796–1818), to satisfy his opulent tastes. The fantastic building no longer exists, but it was an extraordinary example of

re-created medieval grandeur. It was also an unprecedented example of the Victorian interiors to come. Despite superb Gothic depiction, other periods and styles were juxtaposed in the creative, yet confusing, eclectic mode. Beckford's interiors displayed a mixture of fittings, furniture, paintings, and objects from every period. Curtains and draperies had been widely used in Regency times, but Beckford outdid other interiors, with one room clad in purple curtains fifty feet long. Like many late

Right The allegorical figures of Peace and Plenty were perhaps most famously used by Inigo Jones on a design for a fireplace dating from the first half of the seventeenth century. His drawings for the design have survived, and many Victorian fireplace designs were derived from them. This is a reproduction of one of those Victorian designs.

Far right Persian rugs, candlesticks, pictures, and a clock make the hearth the focus of the room.

Victorian homes these rooms had the potential to feel very claustrophobic. However, an illusion of space was created at Fonthill Abbey by the careful positioning of dramatic lighting and overmantel mirrors.

People were generally more widely traveled in the nineteenth century; as a result ideas from Egypt and the Far East were also used for their color and variety. Sphinx heads incorporated into fireplace designs became popular after Napoleon's campaigns in Egypt. Unfortunately, the cultural and period influences were often inaccurately represented, and poor imitations and strange confusions of classical, Gothic, and Oriental styles pervaded middle class interiors until the 1880s.

Advanced techniques in mass production affected every field of the decorative arts. Only the wealthy could afford the originality of fine craftsmen; the ever larger public adopted the misinformed motifs and forms churned out by machine in a wide variety of materials.

By the midnineteenth century most cities had become engulfed in fog as the chimney stacks on monotonous rows of houses belched out smoke.

Early chimneys were very wide, but as coal came into general use chimney flues were narrowed and the chimney pot was added for greater efficiency. Sometimes the chimney flue was as narrow as 9 inches (23 cm), so the deposited soot built up thick and fast and was difficult to clean. Some people overcame the problem by throwing burning hay down the chimney and allowing the

whole structure to catch fire to burn up the creosote. These drastic measures often set the entire house alight in the process. Chimney sweeps had been employed for some time, and in 1788 Jonas Hanway's bill in parliament provided better conditions for young apprentices, who now had to be over eight years old. This terrible abuse of child labor saw many children blackened, rubbed raw, or even stuck fast in chimneys until their death. Finally, with the help of Kingsley's illustrations of the sweep Grimes and his child assistant in *The Water Babies* and a royal commission, the 1875 parliament abolished the right to employ children as chimney sweeps. This was only instigated after 150 years of miserable exploitation, however.

Stricter regulations were enforced on chimney construction, and the danger of fire was reduced by the almost exclusive use of insulating marble, cast-iron grates, and tiles.

Experiments in fuel efficiency led to register grates with dampers to control drafts and the supply of air to the fire. These were cast in one piece as part of the inner frame and back of the hearth and then inset into the marble or timber surround.

By the middle of Victoria's reign, iron founders had produced some very complex designs. Cast-iron grates that had been rectangular for more than 200 years were now cast in semicircular arch shapes as well. In 1875 amazing feats in cast-iron work were portrayed in the Coalbrookdale catalog, and by the end of the century there seemed to be as many designers as there were designs.

Right A Louis XV cast-iron surround painted white, with a horseshoe shaped insert and gleaming brass accessories.

To re-create the feel of a Victorian fireplace the whole room, with all its clutter and confusion of colors, carpets, drapes, and dried flowers, should be taken into account. The well-to-do Victorians set their fireplaces in overdecorated and overfurnished rooms. Walls were papered with elaborate wallpapers or vibrant painted panels, and the comfortable but somber furniture was heavily draped. The Victorians had a passion for covering things. The restraint in women's dress was mirrored in interior decoration styles. The legs of tables were covered and mantelpieces were covered with gold-fringed velvet. One wonders how they would have regarded our stripped pine fireplace surrounds and interiors, as timber was always concealed, usually beneath white paint.

Marble was still used for the best fireplaces. The particular color affects the mood of the room, and if you are planning to reinstate a marble fireplace you should choose the color carefully. Carrara (Sicilian) marble can look far too blue and cold against cream swag curtains. Clean, creamy white marble suits a large room and is quite rare, whereas the blue-veined variety is more commonly available and cheaper. Dark brown or salami-colored marble, with dark timber or the early black lacquer furniture, can create a very somber feeling.

The carpet in a room should meet the edge of the marble surround, and by choosing a carpet of a lighter or darker hue you can create a visual break to maintain the focal point of the fireplace. However, do not attempt to coordinate the color of the marble precisely with your furnishings. Every slab of marble is different, and therefore this is a virtually impossible task!

Consider the shape of the fireplace, too. A Louis XV marble fireplace looks better in a room with swag curtains as it can be difficult to blend

Below left This very large antique Louis XVI-style French marble mantel is carved with acanthus corbels and the center frieze is decorated with crossed laurel sheaves.

Below Blue-veined marble can produce a cold effect in a room. Here, however, a warmer and lighter impression is conveyed by the original Victorian wallpaper that decorates the room.

Below The stone fireplace with its plain Tudor arch is set against white paneling, a William De Morgan-style plate hangs above. Standen House, Sussex, England, was designed by Phillip Webb, who worked closely with William Morris.

Right The Arts and Crafts Movement favored painted paneled walls, green being a particularly popular color. Webb's dining room fireplace is derived from sixteenth century designs. However, the decoration on the burnished cast-iron insert was his embelishment.

curves with square lines. The size of the fireplace should always be scaled to the size of the room. Reception areas usually displayed a grand fireplace, whereas in bedrooms they were smaller and prettier. Those in the least important rooms were very small and simply designed. The degree of ornament on a fireplace related directly to the social importance of that room. In wealthier homes the firebasket was surrounded by ground and polished steel plates framed with brass moldings, grates had decorative engraved fronts in polished steel, and fenders were engraved. Brass accessories were lavish. Toward the end of the century marble became too expensive for the majority of homes and painted pine and mahogany, slate, and cast iron were most common. Ornament became heavier, and tiles and marble insets were used to break up the cast iron and heavy surround. Ceramic mass-produced and hand-painted tiles were a characteristic feature of the age. Even fully tiled fireplaces began to appear.

Compartments to display the beloved bric-a-brac of the Victorians were divided by thin, spirally turned balusters. Norman Shaw, an architect and designer who revived the Queen Anne style, also designed impressive stone hooded fireplaces in the Tudor style. The nostalgic yearnings of the Victorians started a separate fashion: developing from the fashion for stone, timber, and wide hearths emerged the romantic Arts and Crafts Movement.

The Arts and Crafts Movement

Out of all the historic, mass-produced clutter, a group of artists broke away in search of design reform. Two of the instigators, Owen Jones (1809–74), who launched the *Journal of Design and Manufacturers*, and Henry Cole, head of the South Kensington Museum, which later became the

Victoria and Albert Museum, built the foundations of the movement. Cole was involved in planning the Great Exhibition of 1851, and both men wanted to improve the standards of mass-produced designs. William Morris (1834–96), poet, designer, and theorist, became the focus of the movement they had inspired. Morris looked to the simple, traditional English cottage or country farmhouse of the sixteenth and seventeenth centuries and reacted against the Industrial Revolution, advocating the use of local materials and skilled craftsmen.

In 1859 Morris commissioned Phillip Webb (1831–1915) to design The Red House for himself and his wife. This building alone had a profound effect on domestic architecture. The fireplace was a combination of both Webb's and Morris's ideas. It was constructed of exposed red brick that did not

emulate any particular period, although some sections of the brick were laid in a herringbone pattern reminiscent of the early medieval style. Above all, however, Morris rejected specific period detailing. Toward the top the brickwork formed a narrow shelf on which to display the once again fashionable delftware and willow pattern plates. The fireplace gave the room a down-to-earth, comfortable feel.

During the 1870s and 1880s, hundreds of thousands of homes emulated this style, incorporating oak beams, inglenooks, and wrought-iron fire baskets. Ironically, Morris designed homes mostly for the wealthy, mansions in the cottage style. His philosophy, however, was to work toward enabling the ordinary person to enjoy fine design and craftsmanship. "What business have we with art

Right Decorated with ceramic plates, candlesticks, and a clock, with the addition of William Morris-style printed textiles, this fireplace at Standen, the house designed by Phillip Webb, is characteristic of the Arts and Crafts Movement.

at all unless we can share it?" he asked. Most wealthy people ignored the Arts and Crafts Movement, preferring the opulent French eighteenth century styles.

The main difference between the feel of a Victorian room and one belonging to the Arts and Crafts Movement was that the latter was lighter, less ostentatiously elegant, and less cluttered and there was more concern with the use of color. A dark, dull green paint became synonymous with these interiors and exteriors and replaced mahogany and oak-paneled fireplace surrounds. A wooden picture rail ran around the walls linked to the chimneypiece. Heavy draperies and furniture disappeared, as did the large overmantels cluttered with sentimental bric-a-brac. Anything oriental, especially Japanese,

was very much in vogue. The style was understated and well conceived.

By the end of the century design books and periodicals, with all the information needed for learning how to decorate a house, became available. These represented an attempt to educate more people about interior design and decoration ideas. As a result home comfort and improvement flourished.

Cooking ranges, boilers, and primitive central heating systems were developed. Some fireplaces were fitted with small back boilers, giving the fireplace a new use and importance. On the other hand, the increasingly widespread use of gas and electricity signaled that the days of the open fire were drawing to a close.

Left Brass accessories surrounding a fireplace catch the flicker of the flames. With late-Victorian designs no amount of clutter looks incongruous; the Victorians decorated and adorned every surface with floral patterns and prints.

Right An original Art Nouveau tiled register insert, dating from 1907. This late Art Nouveau fireplace displays the stylized plant motifs and undulating line that became widely popular in its day.

Art Nouveau (c. 1892–1905)

The life of Art Nouveau was relatively brief, yet it had a strong impact on twentieth century interiors, advancing the modern design movement and creating a truly international style. The foundations of "modernism" were laid by William Morris and the Arts and Crafts Movement, and Art Nouveau emphasized "style," uniting architecture and decoration in a way that had never been attempted before. Sparse yet sensuous decoration was applied to well-proportioned, logical, and functional structures.

Charles Rennie Mackintosh (1868–1928) was the main exponent of this new style, looking to Celtic art and the Scottish baronial tradition as design sources. Most noted of his fireplace designs were inglenooks, which included built-in furniture and were decorated in pastel colors. His stylized ornamentation was made up of abstractions of curves and ovals, appearing at the end of straight lines or squared-off edges. Motifs ranged from stylized fruit, flowers, and other plant forms to chunky columns and festoons. Highly ornate and expressive ironwork became a feature of this period; shiny paintwork and enameled surfaces were also characteristic elements.

The Modern Age

During the Edwardian period a more conventional approach to design was adopted. A natural progression of the Victorian style overlapped with the distinctive Art Nouveau.

Influenced by William Morris, Charles Annesley Voysey (1877–1941) developed the picturesque country home style, comfortable, opulent, and more acceptable to a wealthy public. Voysey was concerned with producing well-designed fireplaces suitable for the machine age. He believed there was an infinite number of ways in which to express the

Left A fireplace need not be in working order to make a decorative detail in its own right. This small Art Nouveau fireplace in a bedroom has been repainted and polished although the chimney has long been blocked up.

Below left An Art Nouveau-style tiled inset with a stripped pine surround. Art Nouveau design has a timeless appeal and is much favored today.

feeling of the hearth through the fireplace surround, and produced cast-iron, pressed metal, wooden, and tiled versions. Nevertheless, he favored minimal decoration, discarding what he termed "the mass of useless ornament." Combinations of blue and white, or green and white tiles adorned Edwardian fireplaces; the fireplace itself became squarer and more functional, often fitted with a gas fire.

World War I halted any further developments to interior design and the fireplace. Following the war, the jazzy, carefree Art Deco style emerged. Like Art Nouveau its life was short. However, its elaborate, stylized motifs left a lasting impression. Wrought iron became more fashionable than cast iron and was decorated, along with wood, with details abstracted from nature, such as rays of sunlight, clouds, birds, and flowers. Dusty pinks, blues, and soft grays made up the general color scheme.

Many designs from the 1930s onward were bland, with more features being mechanized, central heating becoming widespread, and fewer fireplaces being built. Oil, gas, or electric heating systems became more popular over the next few decades; the popularity of the open fire waned. Electricity was an exciting feature in itself, and some fireplaces were designed with recessed lighting incorporated into the surround. Electric bars were set in tiled or mirrored surrounds; function was of prime importance, and designs were geometric and "cold." Tiles in soft shades and with a mottled pattern were fashionable in the 1930s, and the tiled fireplace continued to be popular for the next few decades, changing only slightly in color and pattern.

Developments to the look and function of the fireplace were minimal in the 1940s. By the 1950s adornment and fixed decoration were severely reduced. Although it was the twentieth century that saw the birth of the professional interior decorator, as distinct from the architect, the number of interior design magazines available enabled the majority of people to decorate their own homes. As houses were now basic but well-designed shells, without a chimney, there was more scope for the arrangement of furniture. Personal decisions about decoration were made possible. However, with the rapid pace at which society now chose to live, time spent on creating cosy homes seemed to be neglected. Fireplaces were built of chunky brick, concrete, quarry tiles, or streamlined metal and were devoid of decoration. Styles were often abstract but always functional; as the television became the focal point of the room intimacy faded into the background.

Only in the last decade, since the oil crisis, have people begun to rediscover the qualities of the open fire. A greater awareness of our environment and heritage, combined with our inherent fascination with fire, has meant the return of the traditional fireplace, with its characterful and welcoming appeal.

Above A fireplace with a difference: a design that cannot fail to provoke a response from visitors!

Above A cast-iron fireplace dating from the 1850s Gold Rush years in Australia.

Left Not all modern designs look modern; this inglenook was designed and built in the 1930s by Justus Jorgensen at the small community of Montsalvat, Melbourne, Victoria, Australia.

Above A contemporary canopied fireplace, with a traditional quality conveyed by the warm flagstones covering the hearth, the polished timber, and the muted tones of the brickwork.

North America

When British settlers first arrived on the east coast of North America they must have appreciated the amount of timber available for their use. With this abundance of timber early American fireplaces were massive. However, by the mideighteenth century the amount of timber burned was becoming cause for concern, and as early as 1770 shortages were reported. (Count Rumford, the American statesman, soldier, and inventor, attempted to make the fireplace more heat efficient by altering the shape of the opening.)

Across the country, as more forests were cleared for crops, wood continued to be burned in these extravagantly large fireplaces. Rooms were designed on a small scale to conserve the inefficient fire's warmth. It was quite common for a home to have three or more open fireplaces arranged around a huge central chimney. Hearths were relatively shallow and extended out into the room to radiate as much heat as possible. Open fires in milder climate settlements burnt brush, grasses, and peat, as well as wood.

One of the most important developments to come out of America was the freestanding stove, later known as the "Franklin stove." Benjamin Franklin discovered this method of complete combustion by containing the flames and smoke within the firebox. He also developed one of the first dampers, a sliding door to restrict airflow between fire and flue, as well as a coal burner. Coal was not in common use until the nineteenth century in North America.

Closed stoves, which were fueled by peat or coal, were introduced by German immigrants. Sea coal was imported from Europe, but at a considerable cost, so Appalachian coal was soon discovered, replacing the use of sea coal and wood fuel.

By the turn of the nineteenth century American

designs were accepted internationally for the first time in history. It is interesting to note that fireplaces designed in America with a European flavor came at the time of America's newfound independence. Samuel McIntyre, in Massachusetts, designed beautifully carved mantels, heavily influenced by Adam's festoons, swags, and fruit. He also included the American eagle in the decoration. Walls of wooden paneling began to disappear and were replaced with paint, fabric, and fashionable European scenic wallpapers.

Below A contained fire set in an unusual brickwork surround. Today, many modern designs are multi fuel conversion heating systems that can be fueled by gas or electricity.

Above A cast-iron insert with a Victorian reproduction marble surround. Veined marble is difficult to match; no two pieces are the same. If a section of an original marble fireplace is missing, a specialist marble dealer may be able to help.

The battle of the styles affected America just as it did Europe. However, neoclassicism won the day, with white marble fireplaces becoming very popular in New York homes. Geometric in their designs, fireplaces with marble slabs and mat black slate were highly fashionable by 1840. Versions of the Regency style were adopted, and timber was generally painted in white or cream, although, in addition, contrasts of vibrant red, blue, green, and yellow often appeared around the room. By 1850 the Empire style was very popular, but by the 1880s a new trend for a simpler style created by H. H. Richardson had evolved. Oscar Wilde brought the message of Morris and the Arts and Crafts Movement to America by telling the public in 1882: "Have nothing in your home which you do not know to be useful or believe to be beautiful." It was this way of thinking that resulted in a more modern approach to design.

Frank Lloyd Wright (1869–1959), known as the father of American modernism, created a unique style that blended interiors with their surroundings. Fireplaces were prominent in Wright's work. One striking example is a fireplace constructed on a bed-rock which rises into the room of the house.

Australia

The evolution of the fireplace in Australia followed similar lines to its development in America. However, the bulk of European settlement took place in the nineteenth century, and the land was stripped of its timber for farming, fuel, and shelter pruposes. Early settlers' homes consisted of one or two rooms built from local materials, such as wattle and daub or stone, with bark or timber shingles on the roof. All homes had large chimneys, including the mere shelters for homes that were common in the years of the Gold Rush. Chimneys were constructed of timber slabs,

Below An original Victorian cast-iron stove set in a surround built for a stove. This example is not in working order but makes a striking addition to the room.

Above In small cottages or less important rooms, wood was most comonly used for the mantelpiece. In Australia this was frequently blackwood, a local hardwood.

stone, or rubble, covered with mud on the inside to prevent them from catching fire. Kitchens were nearly always detached from the rest of the house, as the risk of fire was great.

The pioneers gave little thought to decoration; cooking utensils, hanging from an iron bar above the hearth, were often the only accessories.

In the second half of the nineteenth century all kinds of fireplaces and stoves were imported. Stoves were fitted into brick chimneys, which were painted red ocher; the family room fireplace was regularly whitewashed. The Boom period of the 1880s saw traders scouring the world for alluring merchandise to attract gold-rich Australians. No frontier society had ever found itself so well supplied with goods from England, America, and Europe. The 1880s saw fireplaces become far grander and more elaborate in their decoration. Houses in the southern states of Australia were equipped with fireplaces in almost every room. The dining room typically included a dignified black marble mantel; in the drawing room a pale marble was preferred. In less important rooms slate or timber was used. Fireplaces and furniture were frequently made from blackwood, a local hardwood. Thomas Collcutt (1840–1924), an architect working in the Renaissance revival style, designed overmantels with mirrored backs and numerous shelves for the much-loved display of ornaments. By the end of the century the ornate designs had waned and the move was toward plainer, squarer designs.

The trend toward oil- and gas-fired heating appliances during the 1960s and 1970s led to the abandonment of open fires in the cities. A renewed interest in wood fires has followed the fuel crisis, however, and a substantial number of builders and home improvers have begun to revive the hearth. Homes of local stone, timber, or mud brick are now being built in bush settlements and are beginning to

Right An attractive Art Nouveau style cast-iron fireplace with colorful tiles.

Below Mahogany fireplace surrounds became popular in Edwardian times. This example is designed to a standard Georgian style, with the inclusion of the motifs favored by Robert Adam.

merge into the suburban sprawl. With the availability of wood and the interest in energy saving heating systems, such as stoves, the blazing fireplace is once again as much a part of indoor living during the Australian winter as the verandah for the great outdoors in summer.

CHAPTER 3

Above This free-standing, upright stove looks equally at home in modern settings and traditional country kitchens. This example is gas fired.

To many people the stove and the fireplace mean more or less the same thing: heating devices. To others they are quite separate; one is for cooking on and even slaving over, the other is for keeping warm and relaxing by. The difficulty in making the distinction is that there are so many types of stoves, ranging from the highly decorative Scandinavian wood-burning stove to the dual-purpose heating and cooking range such as the Aga, and finally to the modern gas or electric range, which has little in common with the traditional open fireplace.

In recent years the enclosed stove, primarily as a room heater, has made a huge comeback, with a great many designs with different purposes to choose from. Even if a stove's function is to heat a room, however, most have one or two hotplates to enable minimal cooking or boiling of a kettle.

The renewed interest is due to awareness of the need for fuel conservation, increased costs of heating, and, of course, romantic nostalgia. Even if one regards the stove as a purely decorative object or as an antique, there are many interesting styles available, from countries as diverse as Scandinavia, the USA, Canada, France, the UK, and Australia. So, whether you are looking for a stove to suit your contemporary decor, an Art Deco piece, or a fine old example of Victorian craftsmanship, there is a growing market of superbly engineered stoves, both original and reproduction.

Stoves have not only found their way into more and more family living rooms, but have made their way back into the kitchen, where central-heating ranges fit naturally. They have helped to bring back to the kitchen the feeling of homeliness, which the gas and electric cookers of the 1930s onward, helped to reduce. A kitchen stove encourages a family to gather around its warmth, transforming the kitchen

Right An original Victorian cast-iron range made in Australia in the 1860s. A bread oven is built into the wall on the left-hand side of the fireplace.

into a center of activity once again and keeping the person who cooks company while at work.

The earliest fireplaces provided the basic needs of both heating and cooking. In English history, the Normans were the first to design a kitchen as a separate building, with separate fireplaces primarily for cooking. The Normans, who indulged in elaborate menus, had to provide for their tastes with enormous fireplaces, incorporating a stove and oven. The ovens were built under the stone or brick hearths but were later shifted into the side walls of the open fire for baking bread. Ovens, like stoves, have been used by most cultures for many centuries. The Australian Aborigine used ovens for much of their cooking, be it for bread, fish, or emu. The Normans would have based their oven design on the primitive ovens used in Europe. The Chinese also used ovens and stoves called *kangs*. However, in their culture stoves were generally considered a sign of poverty, and the wealthy therefore concealed their use by placing them outside the home or in an adjacent room. For the Chinese stoves were also a source of heat, and they may have chosen to hide their presence, in much the same way as we conceal our boilers in cupboards or basements. The rich Chinese were far more concerned with ornamental effects, and if stoves were to be seen, they were covered with thick, insulating, earthenware tiles decorated with colorful glazes. It was for their decorative value that Chinese ovens became popular in America in the 1940s for use as outdoor barbecues.

During the Middle Ages in Britain, the majority of people spit roasted their meat on firedogs over the central hearth in the humble cottage, or if they did have a separate kitchen, a bread oven was built into one side. The "cloam oven" originating in the Stone Age became particularly popular in

Above Surrounded by original brickwork and resting on a Welsh slate-tiled floor a wood-burning stove is both attractive and heat efficient.

Cornwall. Often just an oval hole within the thickness of the chimney side wall, bread was baked in the residual heat once the oven was hot enough and the ashes had been raked out. In America the Mexican oven was similar in its function for baking bread. The dome-shaped oven made of mud and rock or brick was filled with hot coals until the heat became absorbed to the right temperature, at which point the coals were raked out and the dough put in to bake. Brick ovens heated with wood were later considered superior to any other oven for baking bread, as they maintained a steady moderate temperature. With further improvements to the stove, nineteenth century iron ovens proved to be too hot for baking bread, and anyone who has tried to bake their own bread in one will know its frustrations.

In Northern Europe stoves for cooking and heating were used in the kitchen. The tiled stove was developed by the Germans in the late eighteenth century and Germanic settlements in North America were involved in manufacturing stoves. Ceramic tiles, such as German Hafner ware, were decorated in high relief and generally finished with a monochromatic green lead glaze. The Pfau family produced tiles coated in vibrantly colored tint glazes.

As ovens had been built into one side of the

fireplace or grate, the logical development to unite these two cooking and heating devices finally came in the late eighteenth century. Cast-iron stoves for heating were developed in Denmark and France, but in the rest of Europe and America iron founders began making cooking ranges in the 1770s. Their perfection is attributable to both Benjamin Franklin, whose ideas led to stoves being mass produced, and to the insights of Count Rumford, who criticized the wasteful quantities of fuel consumed in large open grates. He was reported to have commented: "More fuel is frequently consumed in a kitchen range to boil a tea kettle than, with proper management, would be sufficient to cook a dinner for fifty men."

It was the completely closed European stove that Benjamin Franklin adapted in Pennsylvania, and his designs were then imported to England. In 1802 the enclosed stove, with only one burning fire, was first patented by George Bodley. The "Bodley Range" was the ancestor of our modern cooking ranges. In Europe, America, and Australia, the woman of the house and the servant could sigh with relief over the straightforward and efficient cooking that the new cast-iron airtight stove provided. No longer did cooking mean having to toil over the direct heat of an open fire with an array of grills, spits, cranes, and amber-glowing pots, pans, and skillets. One imagines, though, that hours of maintaining and blacking the iron created a new form of toil. In America, cooking and heating stoves came into general use by 1830. By 1850 gas came into use, so

Left This Aga range has been built into a recess in the wall so that it fits in with the surrounding kitchen units. With its four ovens a model like this can be gas- or electricity-fired.

Below The Aga was one of the many stoves shipped to Australia, primarily for cooking purposes. This white-enameled model blends in comfortably against the white washed walls and black and white floor tiles.

along with coal and wood in country areas, these were the main sources of fuel until the advent of oil and electricity.

A great assortment of American and European stoves, primarily for cooking, were shipped to Australia. These original stoves are extremely popular today and include the potbellied stove, Scandinavian stoves, the parlor stove, the box stove, and the combustion stove. Reproduction versions of these are also popular.

Kitchen ranges with an open fire and a crane suspending pots and kettle remained in use throughout the nineteenth century in all countries. However, their inefficiency was a major cause of complaint. There were problems with the efficient closed stove, too, mainly that the heat emitted from iron stoves made the air too hot and dry. If the dryness of the air is one of your complaints, a container of water placed near the stove and acting as a humidifier can alleviate this. Fortunately many modern designs and methods solve this problem. Another disadvantage of the early closed stove (one that has been overcome today) was that they gave off unpleasant fumes, and worst of all, if coal was used, they poured thick, choking smoke into the skies. This was more than a complaint. Through the next century it became a disaster, killing thousands of people in big cities like fog-bound London. The problems ranged from small particles of scorched dust producing an unpleasant and irritating smell to new diseases like "stove malaria" and "iron cough." There were also complaints of "constipation, chest pains, throbbing of temples, vertigo, fullness in the head, confusion of ideas and cold feet." It is now thought that many of these problems resulted from ignorance of how to operate closed stoves and a tendency to overfeed them with fuel. Dampers helped to reduce some problems, as did the first

Right A kitchen can be transformed into the heart of the home once more. Providing a constant source of warmth and the feel of a country kitchen, ranges draw the family back to the traditional center of activity.

automatic thermostat, invented by the American Elisha Foote.

It is thought that all these complaints led to a resistance in Britain to the idea of using the stove as a means of heating in other rooms. It is also quite likely that they were unwilling to give up the open fire as the focal point to living and entertaining rooms, no matter how inefficient it was compared with the stove. The arrival of the closed stove in the kitchen meant the end of the open hearth in the most vital room of the house.

A large number of stoves were used, however, in the eighteenth century, in hallways or where the

light from an open fire was not necessary. The Soane Museum in London has a cast-iron stove designed for a hall by Robert Adam in 1776 and incorporating classical sculpture and a lantern. Robert Adam and James Wyatt designed stoves representing Roman urns or pedestals supporting candelabra or lamps. Decorative features in the ironwork often depicted palm trees or Indian temples, to suggest tropical warmth. Despite their popularity on the Continent, however, stoves were seldom found in rooms of domestic homes in Britain.

Right The vibrant red model of this Aga range has a contemporary style to it and provides wonderful cooking facilities.

Below right This unusual Italian pottery stove is hand decorated; it is a good example of a stove primarily intended for rooms other than kitchens.

One of the advantages of these early closed stoves was the fuel efficiency; generally only twelve to fourteen scuttles of coal were used in a day. Also, having a stove means that the heat efficiency is 70 percent as opposed to the 30 percent heat efficiency in an open fire. A fire in a airtight stove, when properly loaded, can burn for up to twelve hours without the need for refueling. Unfortunately, most older stoves are not airtight. Another benefit to consider is safety. There is no danger of sparks, burning embers, or falling logs escaping, so the closed stove can be left unattended for hours. Modern stoves are really using the same principles as the Roman hypocausts, especially if they have an attached boiler. This whole concept of controlling combustion and retaining heat has preoccupied inventors, designers, and engineers since the early nineteenth century.

In Europe the market has been dominated by stoves from Scandinavia because of their excellent engineering and tasteful decorative qualities. The Norwegian cooking stove of 1869 was the forerunner to the Aga, which was invented by Dr. Gustav Dalen in 1924. Dr. Dalen, a Swedish physicist and Nobel Prize winner, produced the first closed iron range designed on the heat storage principle. These stoves provide good insulation within the ovens and up to 90 gallons (409 liters) of hot water per day; they were introduced to England in 1929.

The now famous Aga helped to re-establish family life within the warmth of city and country kitchens. The Aga seems a natural choice, fitting snugly back into the place of an old combustion stove or cast-iron cooker. It comes in a variety of enameled colors, such as the vibrant red model, and can be fueled by coke, oil, or gas. The Aga is also said to be descended from the Albert Kitchener,

one of the advanced designs of the 1850s. It may be worth viewing the display ranges at the Castle Museum in York, England, to see the evolution from hob grate to enclosed fire.

Most of these stoves draw in cold air from either the room or from outside, thus providing an ongoing supply of fresh air, which is circulated through the casing in the rear of the stove and then released into the room. It may be better to choose a stove that brings in an outside air supply, to avoid drafts and cold spots.

Another alternative is to install a convector firebox, which retains the appearance of an open fire without the loss of heat via the chimney. If you do have a large fireplace but wish to have greater efficiency and think a stove may detract visually from the existing fireplace, a convector fire may be more suitable. However, they have a tendency to smoking problems.

It is extremely important for the proportions of a stove to be in keeping with the size of the fireplace opening and the dimensions of the room. Existing fireplaces incorporating closed stoves often do not complement one another. To begin with they were not designed to fit together; you either had a closed stove or an open fireplace. The stove may jut out into the room beyond the projections of the mantelpiece and create disharmony; the space left around the stove in a large fireplace opening may look odd, giving one the feeling that the stove has been put there quite inappropriately. On the other hand, if the opening is sealed and the stove is placed in front, the very beauty, as well as function, of the original fireplace surround is denied. On seeing a fireplace one automatically expects to see a fire, not a cast-iron stove. So unless the doors on the stove are open, the focus and relationship between the two can be uncomfortable.

Far left Stoves, particularly the old, slow-combustion, wood-burning variety, fit snugly into inglenooks or large fireplace openings, which were originally meant for spit roasting.

Left An early cooking range of burnished cast iron. Such ranges were found in the kitchens of large households and had the advantage of providing several ovens and space for several large cooking pots.

Below The clean, sophisticated lines of this functional white kitchen are not interrupted by the addition of a cooking range. Although they are usually associated with more traditional kitchens, some ranges suit modern environments as well.

However, inglenooks can be an ideal place to site a stove, especially if old seats around the hearth are retained or benches are incorporated to enhance the cosiness of the corners. Trying to reinstate a traditional open fire within an inglenook can present quite a few problems with the chimney, drafts and choice of fuel. Inglenooks themselves have lots of charm, however, and there is usually enough room to play around with the positioning of a stove. The chimney can be sealed off with a metal plate into which the flue from the stove can be connected. However, you should seek expert advice, as not all big old chimneys are suitable for closed stoves.

Remember that a stove can be a decorative feature in its own right as well as a valuable source of heat. Consider positioning your stove where it is a feature, separate from an existing open fire so that it can be lit on special occasions as a decorative addition in its own right. You may decide to set it into a corner with a new, well-insulated flue.

Below An ingenious piece of engineering, this custom-made combination fireplace and stove was designed from an old steel boiler. It cooks food, warms the house, and heats water and is extremely heat efficient.

The ideal stove should give a view of the fire through toughened glass, incorporate a back boiler, and suit the most refined or relaxed living room. Ultimately, however, it must suit your own individual needs and it may be helpful to visit a home show or speak to fuel conservation experts before you approach retail outlets. There are a number of things to consider when buying a stove. It is a good idea to present your stove dealer with a rough floor plan, showing the area you want heated. The store dealer can provide you with the manufacturer's information on heating efficiency, but this is affected by the location of the stove, the room size, and how many doors and windows there are in the room and their size. Efficiency is also affected by the flue and chimney installation and how you operate it. Stoves are usually capable of heating only one or two rooms. They vary in how much heat they radiate and, therefore, how much living space they heat. Other factors that determine a stove's effectiveness are local climate, whether the house is insulated, and the type or amount of fuel burned. Some American brands are designed especially for small rooms or as an addition to an existing heating source and can be used as either an open fire or an airtight stove. Others have secondary combustion chambers that allow any unburnt gases to ignite before departing through the flue, therefore ensuring maximum heat efficiency. The more enclosed the store is, the more efficient it will be. Whether you choose to have the doors open or closed, however, the heat is still distributed by radiation and by the convection of the surrounding air.

At the turn of this century wood-burning stoves were being abandoned in favor of the modern, clean, efficient fossil-fueled stoves. Where wood is available they are returning with an almost fiery fury. For the generation that missed out on the

Above A hi-tech room setting like this suits this compact stack wood-burner.

Left This small reproduction Victorian cast-iron stove set in a fireplace recess has the appearance of burning hot coals. In fact it is gas fired.

Right An unusual and ornate wood burning stove can also suit more formal rooms. Here, placed in a classical white-painted timber surround, the stove provides more heat than an open fire.

wood-burning stove as an integral part of life, toil and all, it is more than nostalgia that motivates their desire for a traditional stove. It is as if people today refuse to be deprived of the experience!

The developments that came with new fuels had advantages as well as disadvantages. The romantic, fairy-tale image of the cauldron suspended over the fire was once the only method of heating hot water. The evolution of the back boiler, often incorporated into stoves, meant a continuous hot water supply and central heating without the worry of switches and thermostats.

In Australia in the early 1900s, gas heaters were replacing chip or kerosene heaters in bathrooms, and the old slow-combustion or black iron wood stoves were superseded by gas and then electricity. The modern appliances were slow to gain acceptance, however. In many country areas they never did, even though the early gas stoves imitated the designs of wood or coal stoves, with similarly elaborate ornamentation, right down to the grease taps. Many people who adopted the gas or electric cookers simply installed them in the old chimneypiece to retain as much of the character as possible. An advantage of this is that the chimney is used as an exhaust duct for cooking smells. Many gas stoves are simply old wood-burning stoves that have been modified and converted to gas and retain their period charm.

Today there are a range of gas-fired stoves with a realistic flame effect. Wood- and coal-burning stoves are also widely available. There are "cottage," "parlor," and Italian ceramic stoves, central heating stoves, and authentic or

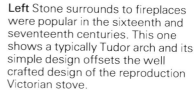

Left Stone surrounds to fireplaces were popular in the sixteenth and seventeenth centuries. This one shows a typically Tudor arch and its simple design offsets the well crafted design of the reproduction Victorian stove.

Left The constant dry heat that a stove provides is used to dry flowers in this uncluttered kitchen–dining room.

Right A colored marble Victorian surround is fitted with a recessed room-heater stove. Its unobtrusive design is appropriate in this setting; a stove jutting out into the room would detract from the original fireplace surround.

Below This contemporary contained-fire stove throws out heat in all directions. Models like this are often multifuel systems. If you are in doubt as to the availability of fuel, a multifuel system could be worth considering.

Left A wood-burning stove, with its doors thrown open to display the burning logs, is almost as appealing as an open fire. With the doors closed the stove is a more efficient heating system.

reproduction stoves from almost all periods.

When you are choosing a stove be realistic about your needs and the availability of fuel. Decorative fuel-effect fires may suit you better. They are inexpensive and easy to light, and there are no ashes to clear up.

Although some stoves are designed specifically for gas, others are designed as multifuel conversion stoves.

A number of late-Victorian stoves had a clean space above the hot plate that was lined with cast-iron carvings or glazed tiles and used for warming plates. Today's stoves are generally made of cast iron, plate steel, or a combination of both. The heavily embossed surface of enameled iron models has the look of old European tiled stoves. You can be extremely creative with tiles; a stove can become even more of a feature by fixing tiles onto a 2 inch (5 cm) thick concrete backing panel within a frame behind the stove. If you are interested in restoring your home to a 1930s look, coke- and anthracite-burning stoves were the vogue of the time. The Cozy Stove Co. produced some with polished steel plates fixed into a cast-iron framework, decorated and finished in gold lacquer. Brick was used then instead of glass, and these stoves were usually found only in kitchens, studios, and workshops.

There are some popular French stoves, such as the Godin and others, that have copied the nineteenth century look.

CHAPTER 4

Above This 1880s Belgian rouge marble fireplace set among a confusing array of other patterns, colors and materials would appeal to the most eclectic designer.

The desire for freedom to create our own vision of the world is as strong as the desire to hold onto the past, which is proven and familiar and therefore secure. To become individuals we need a secure base from which to test our wings. We cannot deny our heritage, nor do we wish to sever the essential bond with our predecessors' thoughts, feelings, dreams, and achievements. Yet, as a modern, developing society we are out on a limb. So much of the future seems threatening, remote, and alien. We are indeed in a decade of compromise. While our minds want to race ahead, we all have a yearning for tradition and now recognize the need for conservation more than ever before. Conservation is more than a passing fashion and indicates a natural respect for the past.

Trends throughout this century, in particular postwar rebuilding programs and the fashions of the 1960s and early 1970s, have led to acts of architectural vandalism. Although we should ultimately aim to leave a legacy of greater quality and a balanced thread of our whole existence, much of our history has been lost through ignorance.

Links with the past are preserved through literature, art, and architecture. The home, be it an architecturally designed showpiece or basic, humble shelter, is like an exoskeleton, our shell to retreat within, our protective castle. That so many people today are buying older homes in the cities and rural areas, reinstating the original or simply "Old World" character, throws light upon our modern society. Other times never yearned for earlier traditions as much as we do today.

It would be virtually impossible for architects and designers of the past to realize their dreams today because in this age time means money, and money means quantity. The quality of traditional craftsmanship, attention to detail and desire for beauty have all but disappeared. Although our

Below The combination of contemporary interior and Victorian fireplace can work well. This reproduction white cast-iron surround is offset by a burnished cast-iron insert and grate.

Right This late-Victorian fireplace is based on a typically French design. The overmantel mirror is a Victorian version of the rococo style.

Below This plain painted wood surround, a restrained element on its own, is offset by striking late Victorian tiles inset in a cast-iron surround and makes a feature of the fireplace.

Bottom This Victorian arched inset, dated *c.* 1840, gives a softer line that contrasts with the more severe pine surround.

recollections of the past may be of solidity, caring, and homeliness, which many modern interiors lack, we cannot simply recreate the image of the past. Our technological age has educated us to be more concerned with how productive and how functional things are, and in any renovation or restoration compromises are bound to be made.

Once you have grasped a feel for the period of your home, it is then a matter of practicalities. Most people want to make efficient contemporary use of the building possible. In this chapter we look at the various considerations to take into account when you are renovating your fireplace. This may mean retaining the period fireplace as a feature but changing or adding to the room another source of heat for comfort, economy, and efficiency reasons. Renovating also means adapting. It could be that your house is a structure with nothing left of the bygone era you are seeking to restore it to; perhaps you live in a modern house but want to create a nostalgic atmosphere. Ultimately, however, your home should respect the original design of the building while reflecting your own character.

Restoring the feel of a place is important. You may actually need to demolish part of the existing structure if it is not in keeping with the period, or you may need to replace sections. The aim is to recover accurately the original form and detail of the fireplace design. For more than a decade now the renewed interest in our heritage has meant that the description "many period features retained" has beome a major selling point in real estate agents' windows, effectively ousting the description "modernized." Beware, however, because "many period features retained" can cover a multitude of sins! The seemingly "cheaper" old house with "lots of potential" can turn into a costly exercise and even a nightmare for people without much knowledge but with lots of enthusiasm!

Above This fluted surround, decorated with classical eighteenth century motifs and dogtooth molding would have been painted white in its day. Today, the austere line is softened when the paint is stripped and reproduction delftware tiles and French flagstones are included.

Very few interiors have retained all their original architectural details, fittings, furnishings, or decoration. Each period had its unique features, the most distinctive being the fireplace, but sadly, even in the hands of well-meaning restorers, the fireplace has suffered more than other features. If the fireplace has been removed or altered, it affects the essential character of a room because rooms were usually designed around fireplaces. Even though fireplaces have been ripped out by generation after generation wanting the latest heating device, large quantities of eighteenth and nineteenth century stock have survived. Good period reproductions have also flooded the market.

You may need professional help in interior design, construction, installation, and purchase. You will need to know about building and safety regulations, and the chapter on renovation and restoration, beginning on page 128, will provide you with the information you need to be aware of when embarking upon any refurbishment.

Initial Considerations

The decision you make in choosing and installing an appropriate fireplace is very important. There are all the aspects of location, design, function, cost, and availability to consider before you arrive at this decision. Putting in a fireplace sympathetic to the architectural style of the house will enhance the feel and value of your home. After deciding on the period, it may be possible to investigate neighbors' homes or similar homes that have not been modernized. This will help you to determine the most suitable fireplace, and with this in mind, you can begin to look at what is available on the market.

An important question to ask yourself is what your reasons are for wanting a fireplace. Do you want it to be the focal point of the room, an additional visual attraction, or just a necessary

Below One of the massive fireplaces with hand-carved red gum timbers built in Australia during World War II.

source of heat? What is the size of the room and the purpose of the fireplace? Will it be in a large room where you entertain guests, or will it be shared only by the immediate members of the family in a smaller, cosier room? How often will you light the fire? Will you have a real fire, or will it be a decorative fuel-effect fire. Consider your life-style and what type of heating appliance would be most appropriate.

Location

If no fireplace or chimney exists, the location depends on the structure of the entire room. You first need to consider whether it is feasible to put in a chimney at all. If your house is suitable, will it be an external or internal chimney, will it be set against a long wall, centrally located, placed in a corner, or placed as a room divider?

In a large room a centrally located fireplace provides the most efficient heating. A freestanding room heater or stove radiates heat in all directions. It will give you a wide range of location possibilities and, with the availability of factory–made flues, it can be positioned almost anywhere. The disadvantages are that you will lose floor space and find it more difficult to arrange furniture. You may wish to make the fireplace the prominent feature of the room, but remember to consider what other focal points, such as the television, will be introduced to the room. A central open fire with a suspended hood is more sensitive to drafts from doors than a fireplace positioned against a wall.

A wall fireplace helps to break up the monotony of a long wall in a large room. You may wish to construct the chimney and the whole depth of the fireplace within the room, on the inside wall. A chimney on an inside wall saves up to 25 percent of heat compared with one on an outside wall. The best position in a long, narrow room is in the center of the longest wall. This way, furniture can be arranged so that the maximum number of people can sit around the fire and enjoy its warmth. If you choose an end wall, seating will be more difficult and the heat may not reach the other end of the room.

If your home has an inglenook it may need extensive renovation. Where the main beam or mantel has been removed, it is possible to install another oak beam or iron girder. It pays to seek professional advice on the condition of the chimney breast as, without care, there is a danger of weakening the brickwork and entire structure. The brick lining is often painted over or plastered to conceal its faults, and if you are replacing bricks, choose old bricks or a type of brick that complements the original. The addition of a cast-iron fireback in a period design has the advantage of protecting the brickwork.

Below A severe and functional contemporary fireplace can create a striking effect in design terms. This example includes a decorative fuel-effect heating system, powered by gas.

Bottom The reeding on this pine surround makes an unusual decoration, bound with ribbons in the carving. Its insert is a typical Victorian horseshoe style. The decorative fender gleams against the blacked cast-iron insert.

Inglenooks are well suited to large rooms. They can help to break up an overly-large room and provide a cosy area that a large room normally lacks. Within the deeply recessed fireplace you can have an open log or coal fire, a decorative fuel-effect fire, or a wood-burning stove, but as much of the heat from an open fire in an inglenook is lost up the chimney, the installation of a stove may be more efficient.

No longer is it difficult or expensive to transform a cold room with a bare open fire into a wonderfully radiant, heated room. If a fireplace exists and looks attractive but does not heat the room well enough, you can install a high-output back boiler capable of heating up to five radiators behind the present fire.

A fireplace positioned in a partition wall can divide the space in a very large room; this also creates the possibility of having two fireplaces placed back to back. However, if you make this choice, the two fires will draw better by having separate flues. In this way a large room can be divided into sitting room and dining room or dining room and kitchen, where both sides benefit from the radiated warmth. On the other hand, if this kind of fireplace already exists and you wish to make the room larger or turn two rooms into one, the dividing wall can be demolished, leaving only the chimney. To convert two back-to-back fireplaces into one large, central fire, some modifications must be made. The degree of reconstruction depends on the height and position of the chimney and the flow of air in the room. For the fire to draw properly the throat may need to be redesigned to encourage an upward draught.

If you intend to locate a fireplace in a small room, it may be possible to construct a chimney on the outside wall so that the entire fireplace recess does not intrude. The fireplace looks less conspicuous

Left Dating from the 1880s, this Australian fireplace is made entirely from painted cast iron. Its imposing Victorian classical design suits the austere masculine billiard room it was built for.

Right Contemporary fireplaces have dispensed with surrounds and mantels. Attention is focused on this example through the addition of a raised and extended hearth acting as a shelf or, perhaps, as somewhere to sit.

Far right Where timber is readily available as fuel, a large fireplace like this unique medieval design is ideal for warming both downstairs and upstairs rooms.

this way. Corner fireplaces take up the least amount of room, but they may not provide a focal point or space enough to gather around the fire.

The position of the fireplace in relation to doors affects the fire's performance. A fire too close to a door can produce drafts that cause smoke to billow out into the room, and a fire opposite a door that opens to the outside is sensitive to sudden gusts of wind when the door is opened. This too causes smoke problems.

The Emphasis

The next aspect to consider is the size of the room. The fireplace you choose must be in proportion to the dimensions of the room. If you have a 20 x 30 foot (6 x 9 m) room with 12 foot (10 m) ceilings, your fireplace should be on a larger scale so that it does not look lost in the room. When a small surround exists in a large room, adding 3 inches (75 mm) to its base or frieze may be enough to make it fit with the room. There are also a number of ways to *reduce* the size of the room or the fireplace, visually. For example, a picture rail can help to bring the ceiling height down. Strong vertical lines appear to raise a low ceiling; strong horizontal lines help to widen a narrow room.

The visual line of the mantel can be tied in with other elements, such as shelving, windows, cabinets, and furniture. A heavier mantel, with fluted frieze grooves running vertically, makes the fireplace look taller, whereas reeding or horizontal lines make it look wider. Above all, you should aim to match the proportions of the fireplace with those of the room, remembering that the fireplace should

look as if it has always been there.

Always consider the ceiling height. If you hang pictures too low above the mantel and on the surrounding walls, the ceiling height is visually reduced. In deciding on the height of the mantelpiece, work out what you are going to place above it (for example, an overmantel mirror, a clock, or vases and ornaments). A mirror should be placed 3 to 6 inches (75–150 mm) above the mantel; a picture 6 inches (150 mm) above, or higher. Usually there is more of a risk in lowering the proportions too much.

The Overmantel

Before the inclusion of an overmantel as part of the fireplace design, textile hangings, a painting, or a carved tablet was positioned above the fireplace opening on the interior chimney wall or chimney breast.

In the sixteenth century the fireplace design incorporated a highly decorated overmantel as part of the chimneypiece, which extended from the floor to the ceiling.

Christopher Wren introduced a large mirror as part of the overmantel. The mirror greatly increased the amount of lighting in a room. Shelves were incorporated to display china, such as delftware.

In the eighteenth century portable clocks from Germany, Holland, and France and candelabra became popular as display items on the overmantel; by the nineteenth century the mantel and overmantel had become a useful piece of furniture. A wooden frame containing several small mirrors and shelves supported by spirally turned wood,

Right This relatively crude stone fireplace, including a simple grate and metal canopy, looks as if it were built centuries ago yet is only a few decades old.

became a popular way of displaying the typical clutter of Victorian homes. An array of bric-a-brac, china, photographs, cards and letters, a central clock, and flowers all rested on an embroidered, velvet-tasseled cloth. More modern fireplaces virtually did away with overmantels, and a simple mirror or painting was hung above the fireplace opening. Often cabinets were built the full length of the wall and included the fireplace; the focal point of the room had shifted to the television set.

Glass-manufacturing techniques vastly improved from the mideighteenth century onward; it became possible to produce large plates of glass, and the backs of mirrors were coated with an amalgam of tin foil and mercury. By 1840 a thin coat of silver was applied by a chemical process. Perhaps the only piece of advice about restoring old mirrors is: Don't. Having the back of an old mirror resilvered removes the main evidence that it is an antique.

Above "Home is where the hearth is": never closer to the truth than when a fireplace, such as this mud brick one, is located where family and friends can gather intimately around it while enjoying the view outside.

Below It is important to consider the size of the room when choosing a fireplace. Anything larger or more ornate than this simple Victorian fireplace would be unsuitable for a small bedroom.

Right A hole-in-the-wall fireplace with a marble frame and additional brass fittings. The poker, tongs, and brush are a traditional addition to a very modern design.

The Contemporary Fireplace

You may not want the fireplace to dominate a modern setting, so a "hole-in-the-wall" type, with the hearth raised right off the floor, may be suitable. However, it risks looking too much like a peephole if it is surrounded by a feature wall of stone. On the other hand, a huge fireplace of this design looks odd if it is surrounded by a thin, flat frame.

Traditional and very contemporary designs can both suit a modern house. Freestanding fireplaces of all shapes and sizes, with smoke hoods, can be made into strong, sculptural features or can be subtly accommodated in a room where some other focal points are of equal importance. Many contemporary fireplace designs suit older settings, but if an old fireplace that reflects the period of the house does exist, resist the temptation to rip it out and modernize. Simply adapting the throat or grate will make the fire more efficient. In very large open fire recesses, heat loss and drafts are common problems, but these can be overcome by reducing the size of the flue and lining and insulating the chimney.

Installing or rebuilding a chimney can be expensive, but freestanding and prefabricated fireplace and chimney units do not need a foundation and are therefore cheaper to install.

Below A convector firebox with a hood is fitted into a classical mantelpiece. Some models like these can include a back boiler built in behind the visible fire. This provides additional warmth in the room and heats radiators and provides a hot water supply throughout the house.

Left A burnished cast-iron inset to a mahogany surround reflects the light of the fire and gives a glowing warmth to a room. Gleaming brass accessories also help to make a fireplace the focus of a room.

Above This framed peephole fluebox fireplace warms the room but, in design terms, is unobtrusive and compact.

No Chimney

If you cannot afford a new chimney, or if structural problems make it impossible for you to have one, an alternative is to install an artificial gas log or coal fire, which simply requires a flue. Thanks to recent advances in gas fire technology it is now possible to have a real flame gas fire without the need for a chimney at all. With this type of fire the flue pipe can be run up to a convenient outlet in the roof. Because the flue itself is constructed with inner and outer pipes, the outer surface remains relatively cool. It is, of course, essential that the manufacturer's safety precautions and local regulations be scrupulously followed with regard to such matters as clearances between the flue and the ceiling opening, the rise above the roof, and so on. Properly installed, this type of fire is ideally suited to the many homes that were built without chimneys when fireplaces were unfashionable or to flats in large old houses, where the chimneys have been lost in conversion.

Above This burnished cast-iron mantelpiece faithfully reproduces original late eighteenth century design motifs. Its austere and imposing elegance would suit a larger room.

The Surround

The eternal rule of pleasing interior design is that all components complement one another and harmonize with the entire room. Today the market is full of a wide variety of original and reproduction fireplace surrounds and inserts, mainly of the Victorian period. The continually increasing demand has resulted in many shops' specializing purely in fireplaces. The quality, style, and price vary enormously.

It is also worth investigating architectural salvage yards and antique shops, as original cast-iron fireplaces can still be found in various conditions. Most of these can be restored quite easily and cheaply, although they should be checked thoroughly to make sure that they are not warped. Whether buying an original or reproduction, it is best to visit suppliers of good reputation, as they are more likely to advise you on the right style and have a range of stock to choose from. You can also have your own fireplace designed, but obviously it is cheaper to buy a standard design from a large manufacturer.

Most reproduction period mantel designs are taken from the eighteenth and nineteenth centuries. They incorporate typical decorative features, such as fluted columns, ornamental friezes, carved swags, scrolls, urns, rosettes, foliage, fruit, and flowers. The range of mass-produced products varies in quality, and often the decorative details are of too small a proportion to the overall effect.

The choice of materials ranges from painted wood, waxed pine, or mahogany to fiberglass and plaster. If you are looking for an unpainted pine mantelpiece, notice how the color and grain vary among different types of pine. Russian pine is a slow-growing timber and therefore has very few knots. It has a warm, mellow color, whereas other

Below At Christmastime the fireplace comes into its own as the heart of the home, around which the entire family can gather.

Above The raised grate in this fireplace is based on middle to late eighteenth century designs, which displayed neoclassical motifs and elegant curves. The overmantel mirror can help to improve the proportions of a fireplace in a room with a high ceiling.

types can have a greenish tinge. A Russian pine matelpiece with carving can give an antique feel that hardwoods cannot quite match. However, a pine surround does not suit all rooms. It can diminish the grandeur of certain rooms and may not complement the furnishings of other rooms. Oak, stone, or a combination of both might look better.

During the Edwardian period mahogany was the timber most commonly used; a surround of this wood would be the one to use in a 1900s house, if you were trying to restore it in keeping with the period.

The carving on a mantelpiece can give a good indication of the period. Elaborate, curved carving denotes a French or Victorian mantelpiece; refined, geometric detail with classical motifs is characteristic of the eighteenth century, and a heavy slab of timber with simple lines and little detail is reminiscent of an early colonial American fireplace.

Fireplaces are usually installed as part of the

Above A white marble Louis XVI style fireplace gives a spacious and more formal feel to a room. With soft colors surrounding the fireplace, this formality is softened, although the room retains a classical style.

second stage of decoration in a house, along with skirtings, cornices, and picture rails. The mantelpiece is often used to tie the fireplace in with other architectural elements of the room. If you intend to have a painted mantelpiece, purchase it only with an undercoat so that you can match the colors precisely in the room.

The characteristic Victorian fireplace was made almost entirely of cast iron. The size of the hearth, grate, and opening was reduced dramatically and inserted into a richly ornamented opening. Some chimneypieces were made entirely of cast iron, avoiding all combustible materials. By the end of the nineteenth century the artistic movement that sought to defy the Industrial Revolution and revive handcrafted fireplaces had come to terms with machines; improved methods of production and quality were sought. Today's cast-iron reproduction market encompasses a wide range of designs that vary enormously in quality. They vary from the

Right Some convector firebox fireplaces, like this example, are multifuel conversion heating systems. They can contain a real fire, or, alternatively, can be fueled by gas or electricity as decorative coal effect fires.

Below Original versions of this classical surround with fluting and roundels would, in their day, have been painted white. However, today, stripped pine is recognized for its attractive and less austere appeal.

Below A Georgian-style marble surround is matched with a Victorian-style cast-iron insert. Late-Victorian inserts became smaller, and if you are thinking of matching one with an earlier surround, you must take careful measurements as it may prove virtually impossible.

smaller delicate versions to the grandly ornate, consisting mostly of arched, tiled, and "cameo" inserts.

Whether installing a new or secondhand cast-iron fireplace, it is important to choose one with dimensions as close as possible to the existing fireplace opening. Some late Victorian cast-iron inserts are so tiny that they can be impossible to fit into a surround from another period. It makes the job far easier when you do not have to contend with altering the shape of the opening or filling gaps. It is also very important to make the fireplace look as if it has always been there, blending in with the mantelpiece and the overall background.

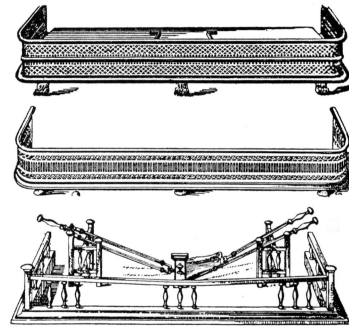

Accessories

The term "fireplace" is all embracing. It includes specific parts, such as the hearth, the grate, the fireback, the back boiler, the stove, and the mantelpiece, overmantel, and surround. Most people add accessories to assist with maintaining the fireplace or simply to decorate it. Today, some of what were once parts essential to the working fire are now redundant and used only as decorative objects.

Equipment for tending the fire, such as shovels, tongs, hearth brushes, and pokers, are obvious accessories to place in a stand on the hearth. Brass or copper containers for storing wood or coal are also attractive.

Below The accessories on this hearth are unnecessary but make an attractive feature.

Right An illustration from a late Victorian book on household management. The author recommended that white marble mantelpieces to be covered with velvet and lace as they were "unsightly in the highest degree." Fortunately, this opinion has not survived.

Coal Scuttles and Log Cradles

A number of attractively decorated containers for storing coal and wood came into fashion during the eighteenth and nineteenth centuries. The most common was the helmet-shaped scuttle made of polished brass, copper, oxidized silver, or painted and lacquered metal; it included a metal liner. Positioned next to the fireplace, these scuttles contained sufficient fuel to top up the dying embers. Some coal buckets had a carrying handle and handle at the back for pouring coal into stoves or onto a fire. A metal basket with two open sides, called a log cradle, was useful for carrying long logs to the fireside; rush and wicker baskets were also popular for storing logs.

Bellows

Originally made from animal bladders ("bellies") or animal hide, bellows were used to encourage sparks to flame. During the Middle Ages a nozzled leather bag with a wooden frame was used. These frames were carved, painted, lacquered, and inlaid or mounted with either bronze or silver. In France, however, bellows were not used. The French preferred elegant fans, which were used for kindling a fire and for cooling one's face from the radiant heat.

The addition of the correct period accessories to a fireplace helps to make the hearth the focus of the home. Antique coal scuttles, bellows, shovels, tongs, and pokers are now collector's items and as well as being finely crafted and decorative are an investment. However, many good reproductions of original designs are now available; among the wide variety there is something for everyone.

Left A stove can be fitted into a fireplace surround very effectively. This Victorian marble surround is off-set by a reproduction Victorian cast-iron stove. Stoves have the added advantage of being more efficient and economical to run and distribute more heat in a room. However, the proportions of stoves are unsuitable for some surrounds.

Right The fireplace in the Great Hall at Montsalvat was built as recently as the 1950s, proof that dreams can still be realized.

Firedogs

Firedogs are the oldest form of domestic fire implements. The earliest examples date back to the Iron Age. Originally they were simple U-shaped andirons for supporting logs in an open fire. They could be raised to allow the passage of air between the hearth and the wood and prevented the burning logs from rolling out into the room.

Firedogs, or double andirons, became a favorite place to display the family crest or other decorative emblems. They were mostly made of cast iron and were adorned with brass and silver only in wealthy households. The various forms of firedog used during the seventeenth century were made of wrought iron with brass ornamental tulips. These designs later incorporated a polished brass ball, which mirrored the glowing flames. Elaborate French and Italian andirons were imported into England at the end of the century, but when coal came into general use firedogs were no longer necessary and were seen merely as a decorative accessory.

In the nineteenth century they were put to use supporting dog grates. However, they were still basically a decorative feature in gilt bronze or cast iron and were designed in rococo, Gothic, neoclassical, and Chinese styles. Firebaskets largely replaced any need for firedogs.

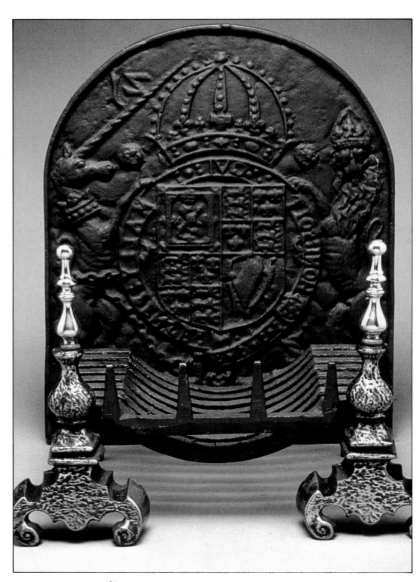

Right A cast-iron grate and built-in fireback. From its origins in the late fifteenth century, the fireback has always been ornately decorated. This seventeenth century-style example is decorated with a coat of arms.

Firebacks

The fireback is an essential part of any fireplace and is a means of radiating more heat while protecting the brickwork behind it. It is also another surface to be decorated. They first came into use at the end of the fifteenth century. The early examples were crudely decorated with patterns made by pressing simple objects into liquid iron in open sand molds. Imprints were made with shells or metal objects, and ropes were used to create a border. Until the midsixteenth century firebacks were greater in width than height, and it was only in the early eighteenth century that they became taller and narrower. The decoration on firebacks in the seventeenth century varied from simple patterns to coats of arms, symbols of trades, caricatures, classical scenes, representations of animals, biblical themes, and topical events. These pictures in the fire reflected political and religious leanings, too. During the religious persecutions of Mary Tudor in the sixteenth century some very gruesome scenes were illustrated. One example depicts Richard Wood, a Protestant iron founder and his wife being burned at the stake. In the eighteenth century firebacks were elaborately decorated in the Flemish or Dutch style. A typical fireback of that period had an arched top and dolphins reclining on either side. As the fireplace became smaller, however, firebacks were incorporated into coal grates and lost much of their individuality and ornamentation. They were eventually replaced by firestone bricks or tiles, which absorbed less heat.

Right An example of the wide range of good reproduction grates available today.

Below and bottom Two examples of reproduction Georgian burnished cast-iron grates.

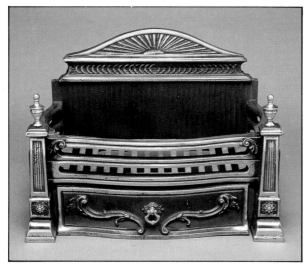

Grates

Grates are not an essential part of the fireplace unless coal is burned. The earliest grates resulted from firedogs being joined together with horizontal bars, often filling the width of large open fireplaces. Smaller coal grates placed in these wide openings often caused smoke problems.

In the cities the use of coal necessitated the raising of the grate to provide ventilation under the fire. Coal must be contained in a compact mass so that enough heat is generated for combustion, and grates may have developed from the charcoal brazier. Dog grates, which had their sides and backs angled, were faced with heavy iron, often decorated on the sides and plain or ribbed at the back. Hob grates appeared in the eighteenth century, set into the fireplace with fire bars flanked by two steel plates, which were usually decorated. These plates were surmounted by hobs, which provided a good place to boil a kettle. The Carron Company and the Dale Company of Coalbrookdale employed John Adam to design many of their hob grates, and he used elegant neoclassical motifs as decorations.

When coal began to supersede wood, the grate was raised about a foot above the hearth and was greatly reduced in size. The register grate was invented in the mideighteenth century to control the flow of smoke and heat. Designed with the back and side plate extending upward to the chimney opening, a moveable iron "register" plate was fitted at the top to adjust the size of the flue opening; the inner back was lined with firebrick. Hundreds of patterns were manufactured, and in the nineteenth century the grate was fitted into a surround of cast iron, polished steel, or tiles.

This page Manufacturers today are faithfully reproducing eighteenth and nineteenth century designs for grates and firebaskets. Some of these copies are well made and look genuine.

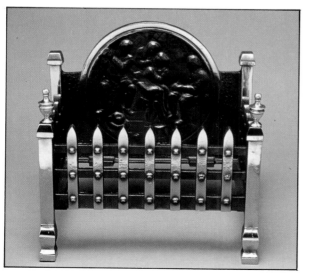

Firebaskets

In the 1600s, when sea coal first came into use, the firebasket was devised to contain it. Early firebaskets were constructed of iron bars on masonry supports, and later cast-iron panels, to stand on a hearth. These were large enough to take logs or coal and had spikes along the top to prevent the logs from rolling off.

Many attractive models were produced toward the end of the seventeenth century, and ornamentation was influenced by the French before the Adam brothers arrived on the scene. In the eighteenth century, a typical firebasket consisted of an opening enclosed by a frame, an apron, side panels, and rounded or bowed bars. Ornamentation continued to be treated in a variety of ways and in great detail, according to the fashion. During the nineteenth century, firebacks, grates, and firebaskets were built into an iron plate to fill the fireplace opening.

When looking for a replacement grate, select one that is appropriate to the style of the fireplace and period of the home. Avoid reproduction grates that are overdecorated for the period. Wood or specific types of coal are recommended for grates, as coke and some types of coal generate intense heat, causing firebricks and cast iron to crack.

Right A fireback depicting a coat of arms in sixteenth century style.

Fenders

Stone curbs around a medieval hearth were the earliest fenders, but the familiar metal guards were introduced with coal grates. They are a highly decorative addition to the fireplace, helping to confine ashes and burning coals and prevent them from falling out onto the floor.

Fenders were made in every fashionable ornamental style, constructed of burnished steel, brass, cast iron, and even silver for the wealthy. They were highly polished and were pierced or decorated with stamped impressions. The fender often matched the apron of the grate; Robert Adam matched it to the overall effect of the decor. In the 1920s tiled exended hearths and curbs were introduced, effectively replacing any need for the decorative metal fender.

Below A Victorian marble fireplace based on a French design and dating from 1891.

Fire Screens

Fire screens are wire mesh screens placed in front of a fire to protect the room from escaping sparks and were generally made up of a forged or brass frame with a black wire mesh and simple decoration.

Much smaller fire screens, hand held and made of wicker or wood, have been used since the Middle Ages to protect the face from the radiant heat. In those early days they usually took the form of a square or shield-shaped tapestry or embroidery, decorated with armorial bearings and attached to an adjustable brass or wooden pole. Large versions stood on either side of the fireplace on tripod bases; smaller ones stood on tabletops. When the fireplace is not in use a fire screen conveniently hides the empty grate or blackened hearth.

Fire Curtains

Fire cloths or curtains came into fashion in medieval times after the disappearance of the hooded fireplace. They were decorative features that served a functional purpose. Suspended from the mantel, the curtain narrowed the opening of the fireplace, increasing the draft and removal of smoke. They were generally made of leather or tapestry, but toward the end of the seventeenth century hinged iron doors were introduced. Wire mesh curtains were used in the nineteenth century to confine flying sparks, and decorative cloths were used purely for ornament.

Canopies

Originating from the hooded chimney piece of the Middle Ages, canopies help to radiate heat and remove smoke in a large open fireplace. Some modern fireplace designs incorporate a canopy as part of the appliance. They are made in galvanized, stainless or enameled steel, aluminum, copper, and brass and are either plain or simply decorated with hammered patterns.

Fire Irons

Shovels, tongs, pokers, and forks came into general use in the 1700s to handle coal. Fire irons with long handles were used in log fires to shift logs and remove ash. In both the eighteenth and nineteenth centuries it was fashionable to display a purely ornamental set of polished brass or steel tools in a stand by the hearth and have another set at hand for practical use. In wealthy homes fire irons with silver mountings often incorporated the family crest. In the twentieth century sets of fire irons have been reduced in size and mainly serve as decorative accessories.

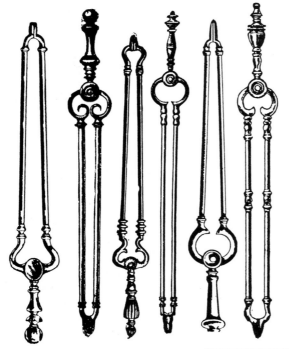

Below This cast-iron fireplace was transported from Britain during the Gold Rush of the 1850s. With it came the entire house (also made of cast iron). On the ship that brought it the iron was used as ballast.

Opening up a Fireplace

The discovery of an original fireplace can be the most exciting and rewarding aspect of restoring an old home. Reinstating the feel and function of a fireplace is giving back to the home its life force and essential character.

Caution is needed in opening up an old fireplace, but with common sense, some good advice, and a little persistence, it is not too difficult to achieve. However, it is worth reading the chapter on renovation and restoration, starting on page 128, before embarking on such a task, as you may discover that major repairs or reconstruction is needed. If this is the case it could save you a lot of time, effort, and money to entrust the job to someone who understands fireplace construction. If you are in doubt or you encounter any problems along the way, do not hesitate to contact a professional.

If you suspect that there is a hidden fireplace, tapping the wall until it sounds hollow may give you a clue. Some fireplace openings are merely covered with a board in a timber frame, so it is simply a matter of prying the frame free; if you are very lucky, the original fire surround may have been simply boarded over and is still intact. Bricked-up openings require more work, and you need to ascertain the presence of a recess called a builder's opening. However, before you start hacking away at the chimney breast, it is wise to determine how the previous occupants may have gone about sealing the chimney. Go outside and have a look at the chimney itself; sometimes it will have been capped with slate or a paving slab, with airbricks underneath. If this is the case, the slab will have to be removed, the airbricks replaced with solid bricks, and the chimney pots put back. Unfortunately, in some cases the chimney will have been removed completely to below roof level. In this situation a builder will have to be called in to rebuild it.

Having established the condition of a chimney, you can begin the process of opening up the fireplace. (Make sure that your room is protected against a heavy accumulation of rubble and dust.) Begin by removing the airbrick or ventilator or by removing two bricks at about 12 inches (30 cm) above the floor. The next step is to hold a lighted candle in front of the hole to ensure that there is an updraft. If the flame remains this is an indication that there may be an obstruction in the chimney or that the chimney has been capped. Alternatively a smoke test can be carried out. This involves lighting a small pellet, which may be obtained from a good plumbing supply store, and placing it in the opening. A great deal of smoke is given off and should travel straight up the chimney and be seen leaving the chimney pot. If smoke escapes from the chimney shaft into the room or elsewhere into the home, you will have to seek professional advice before proceeding. Once you are satisfied that the chimney is sound and free from obstruction, you can proceed to open up the fireplace and reveal the builder's opening. Having accomplished this, now is the time to have the chimney swept. Subsequently you should have it swept at least once a year, even if you are using a gas decorative fuel-effect fire. Your fuel supplier will be able to provide you with a list of sweeps in your area.

This is the best time to have the chimney swept, and your fuel supplier will be able to advise on local sweeps. The chimney should be swept with both brush and vacuum cleaner as vacuum alone is not sufficient.

Before — the fireplace has been fitted with a gas fire.

Once the gas fire was removed, a smoke test was carried out to ensure that the chimney was free from blockages and leaks. A smoke pellet (obtainable from any good plumbing supply store) is lit and placed in the opening. A lot of smoke is given off and should travel straight up the chimney. Check that the smoke is coming out of the chimney pot, and also check the upstairs rooms for leakages. If smoke escapes into the room or elsewhere in the house, professional advice must be sought before proceeding.

Builder's opening diagram.
1. Lintel 2. Back hearth
3. Constructional hearth
4. Superimposed or decorative hearth.

The fireplace can now be opened to reveal the builder's opening. Mark the area that the fireplace will cover, and first remove the plaster to expose the brickwork. Care should be taken at this stage not to disturb the lintel, which supports all the brickwork of the rest of the chimney breast.

Once you have ascertained the position of the lintel, the bricks can be removed using a sledge hammer and a cold chisel, or alternatively, an electric jackhammer, which can be hired by the day, will accomplish the job much quicker.

The builder's opening, now revealed, is still filled with rubble and the remains of the old fireback; this must be removed and cleared away. Some time in the past the fireplace opening was obviously narrowed by the building of brick piers on either side of the chimney, but as these will not impede the new fireplace, they can be left in position.

If a decorative fuel-effect gas fire is to be fitted, the pipe can now be run from the tap into the back of the fireplace; the surround will be fitted over the pipe and it will therefore be much less obtrusive. Safety is all-important when working with gas, and it is wise to employ a licensed professional to install the piping.

The fireplace, minus its mantelpiece and tiles, is now placed in position to check that it is level and that there are no obstructions around the builder's opening to stop it from standing flat against the chimney breast.

Once satisfied that the fireplace fits, it can be removed and the decorative hearth laid. First an even coating of adhesive is painted onto the existing constructional hearth to ensure a good bond between the old and the new cement.

A layer of mortar mix approximately 2 inches (5 cm) thick is then laid and leveled, and quarry tiles are laid on top. To make sure they are flat, check them with a level and then grout with the mortar mix.

The decorative tiles can now be inserted into the frame. Wedge pieces of cardboard behind them to ensure a tight fit at the front of the frame.

The fireback can now be fitted to the surround. This rests on the bottom of the frame and is held in place by a metal band.

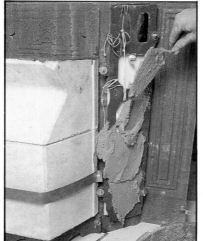

Plaster over the backs of the tiles to hold them securely in position and leave to set.

If there are still any obstructions preventing the fireplace from sitting flat against the wall, tilt it forward and remove them with sledge hammer and cold chisel.

Carefully lift the fireplace (which is by now extremely heavy) into place, taking care not to disturb the newly laid hearth.

The fireplace has fittings on either side, top and bottom, and it should now be bolted to the wall.

The space between the fireback and the chimney wall is now filled with rubble to the height of the fireback. This acts as an insulator and saves heat from being lost up the chimney. Finish this with a layer of cement.

Cement over the bolts and then plaster the fireplace into position.

In the case of a decorative fuel-effect fire, the gas pipe is now surrounded with a layer of cement. This forms a platform for the coal tray to sit on.

The tray is placed in position, and the gas pipe is connected. A layer of sand is poured into the bottom.

The coals are positioned and the fire lit to check that it is working properly. The coals can be rearranged to achieve the most realistic flame effect, but the fire should not be left alight for more than about ten minutes. It is best to wait for three days to give the wet plaster and cement time to dry thoroughly; otherwise cracking results.

The fireplace installed and working.

An alternative to a fire surround is to tile the inside of the builder's opening and install a stove. In this case an original Victorian Godin stove has been renovated and provides a very efficient and attractive source of heat.

DESIGN OPTIONS

These pages A selection of fireplace tiles based on original Victorian and Art Nouveau designs.

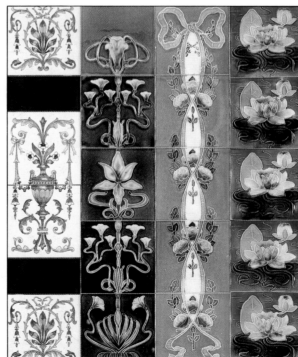

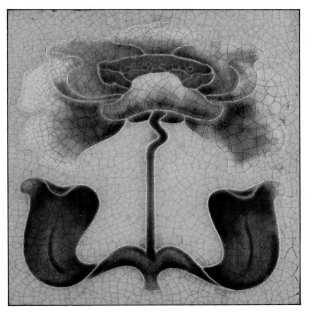

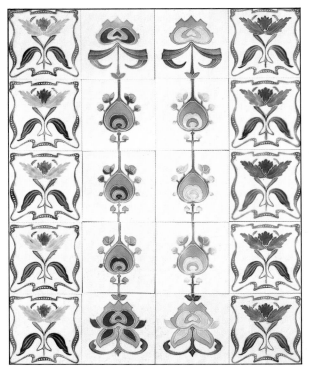

CHAPTER 5

The main aim of restoring a fireplace is to create the feeling that it has always been part of the room. Whatever alterations or repairs need your attention, you want the finished job to appear professional. With a few simple step-by-step techniques you can achieve this and solve a range of problems associated with the chimney or hearth and the restoration of the more visible features, such as the mantelpiece.

The installation of a new fireplace where none previously existed is a relatively safe and simple matter, providing you follow the appliance manufacturer's recommendations and the appropriate building regulations. It becomes more complicated and costly if you don't have a chimney or if your chimney is in need of repair.

As an alternative, prefabricated metal chimneys or flue systems, which include both structure and lining, are simple to erect and far more economical. Before installing a flue in an existing chimney have it professionally cleaned and checked. Cracks in flue liners and mortar between bricks or a buildup of soot can cause fires.

For an open fire with a firebox that is between 24 and 28 inches (61–71 cm) wide, the flue width should be 12 inches (30 cm). The Brick Institute of America has established recommendations for openings up to 96 inches wide and 40 inches high (244 cm x 102 cm) with fireboxes up to 76 inches wide by 40 inches high (193 cm x 102 cm). In all cases, the recommendations of the manufacturer and local regulations must also be carefully followed. Square flue liners are ideal for chimneys as only their corners fill with soot, leaving the center clean for a longer period of time than round flues.

For gas-fueled fires, special flexible stainless steel liners are available, but they are not suitable for open fires. All stainless steel flues should last for at least twenty years.

As the chimney may not have been used for some time, it must be carefully checked. Very early chimneys should be thoroughly scrutinized. Some of these are worth reconstructing, but because of their high combustibility it will be necessary to install a flue. Chimneys in their exposed positions can suffer damage from the effects of rain, wind, and frost. Therefore it is absolutely vital to ensure their

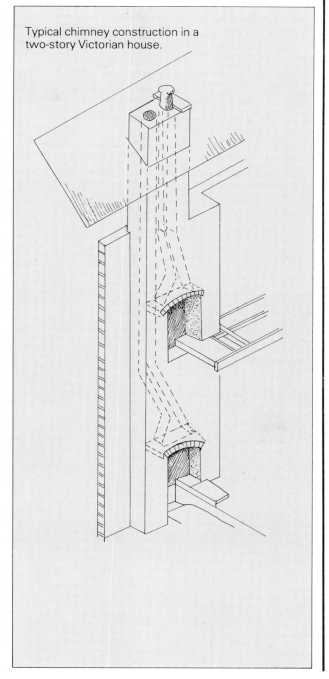

Typical chimney construction in a two-story Victorian house.

structural stability and to make sure that mortar joints are intact.

Old chimneys were generally built with wide bases to accommodate large fireplaces. Recurrent modernization and attempts to cure smoking problems may have altered the size and opening of the fireplace. Indiscriminating renovators have often removed part of the original structure without any regard for safety. In these cases, and in the case of any major structural work, inspection should be carried out by a specialist.

One problem that may be encountered is a chimney that has developed a lean. Chemical attack from slow-combustion stoves and room heaters can cause this, or it can be the result of weather damage.

Insufficient foundations, faulty construction, design, or materials, and movement, which is often inevitable in old buildings, may all be possible causes. Very high chimneys are more prone to leaning as a result of constant weather changes, and these should be stabilized or lowered and reconstructed. If the lean appears below the roof line, it is possible that the chimney beam has shrunk or become damaged by woodworm, fungus, or rot. Anything placed on the chimney, such as a television antenna or weathervane, will eventually cause the chimney to lean, as will corrosion and fractures. Reconstruction may be the only solution if the damage or lean is severe, but explore the possibility of stabilization first.

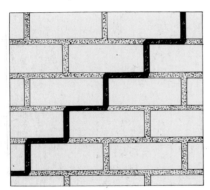

Fracturing of brick or stone is often caused by weather damage. If the cracks follow the lines of the joints and are not extensive, all that is necessary is repointing.

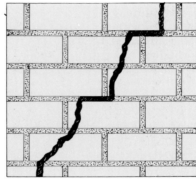

If the cracks actually cut through the bricks these will have to be replaced. If the damage is extensive the stack will have to be rebuilt.

Rake out the old loose mortar to a depth of at least ¾ inch (20 mm) with an old screwdriver. Do not use a hammer and chisel as this could result in cracked bricks. Brush away any loose material, and soak all the joints to be repointed with water.

Cracks in chimney masonry are another problem and can occur for a number of reasons. Faulty design, alterations, and chimney cleaning with heavy chains and weights are just some. Frost can also have a detrimental effect, especially if water has seeped into the masonry. Fractures that run along the joints can be fixed by correct repointing, if the damage is not extensive. If the bricks themselves are cracked they should be replaced. If fractures cover a substantial area, however, complete rebuilding may be necessary.

An unused chimney may have been capped to prevent birds and rain from entering. Remove the capping, and check that the chimney is complete. If the chimney has been demolished to below the roof level, you must build it up again with new brickwork, following the style of similar period examples. The height of the chimney, flue, and chimney pot is important to restoring a good working fire (check local building codes for terminal elevation requirements.) The tapering shape of a chimney pot not only adds an interesting decorative touch but increases the velocity of escaping smoke and gases, reduces the effects of downdrafts, and minimizes the entry of rain. Square-based pots that gradually taper to a smaller round diameter at the top provide a much smoother passage for the gases. Chimney pots should be fitted securely, made airtight, and be the same size as the flue, if one exists.

Mix the mortar and press into the brick joint until it is firmly packed and protrudes beyond the bricked surface.

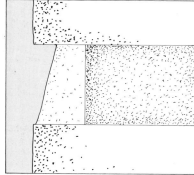

To ensure that rainwater cannot collect in the joint, the mortar is sloped down and outward. Use the edge of a pointing trowel to press in the mortar ⅛ inch (3 mm) at the top of the joint.

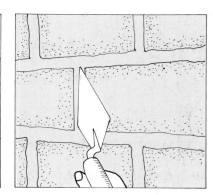

Starting with the vertical joint, hold the trowel level with the right-hand brick and press in at the other side.

The chimney should be thoroughly inspected for any defects and cleaned by a reputable sweep using a rod and brush as well as a vacuum cleaner. Vacuum sweeping alone is not usually sufficient. Once the fireplace is unblocked and restored to working order, a chemical cleaner, which contains a desooting agent, is available for solid fuel, gas, or oil appliances. Sprinkled onto the hot fire, it forms a gas that reacts with the carbon in the soot and peels away the buildup.

The type of fuel burned affects how often the chimney should be cleaned and checked. As coal produces a lot of soot, coal-burning fires need cleaning two to three times during a winter. Wood fires, especially if the timber burned is young or wet, cause a buildup of tar, which is not easily dislodged with a brush. The chimney will need sweeping twice a year to remove the flaking and burned cinders. Flues for smokeless fuel should only need to be cleaned once a year, but the throat of the heating appliance must be brushed at least once a month. A flue attached to a stove needs to be cleaned more frequently than the chimney of an open fire. Bends in flues enable pockets of soot to accumulate, and a buildup of soot in a flue decreases the efficiency of the draft and cause smoke to spill into the room. The first signs of a buildup of soot are either small puffs of smoke entering the room or soot itself dropping onto the fire or hearth. In addition to soot buildup, deposits of creosote can form in the top part of

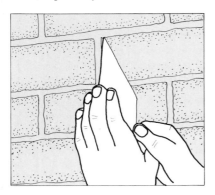

Draw the trowel down the end of the brick, and cut off the surplus mortar with the trowel edge.

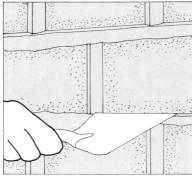

On horizontal joints press in to a depth of ⅛ inch (3 mm) at the top of slope to the bottom edge.

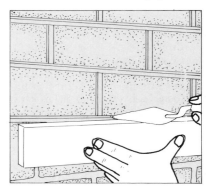

To remove surplus mortar, hold a straightedge below joints and trim with the trowel. When the mortar is almost dry, lightly brush the surface of the joints.

Wood

Though nothing quite rivals a traditional wood fire, the use of wood as fuel has created much ecological imbalance, with forests throughout the world fast disappearing. Another point to consider is that the burning of wood is subject to strict regulations in certain areas.

The type of wood makes a difference to how the fire burns and radiates heat. Hardwood burns better than softwood and leaves little ash, whereas softwoods burn with lively flames but produce a lot of ash. They also burn quicker than hard woods and send out more flying sparks.

A drawback with wood as a fuel is the need to find space to store it, as it should be kept fairly dry.

"Artificial logs" are widely available in supermarkets and hardware stores. Made of compressed solid fuels, they are long-burning, relatively clean, and quite expensive.

Coal

Coal also has a long association with the fireplace, but only since the Industrial Revolution has it become the main source of fuel. Unlike the other fossil fuels there are still plenty of reserves, though it is predicted that coal will only last another three hundred years.

Coal is one of the cheapest fuels and is produced in various forms, each with their own burning characteristics that suit specific types of fire appliances. There are two main types: bituminous, which produces an abundance of soot and ash and is therefore better used in an open fire than a closed stove; anthracite, which is relatively smokeless, suitable for both an open fire and a closed appliance. In the USA today, anthracite is used in stoves, but is rarely burned in fireplaces.

Decorative fuel-effect fires

These fires are not designed to be the primary source of heat; they are used alongside a central heating system to provide the appearance of a coal or wood fire at a low cost. They are often sold as a package which includes the fire surround and the cost of installation. But, there are also models available that fit any fireplace and can be made to measure. In addition, to suit a large fireplace, they can also be used in free-standing firebaskets.

Efficiency can be increased by fitting a decorative fuel-effect fire into a convector box, which is a double-skinned metal box. Heat from the fire is absorbed into the metal and transferred to the air, setting up convection currents on the same principle as a radiator. There are also specially built airtight stoves which take decorative fuel-effect fires, but you cannot fit one into an existing stove. Safety is of the utmost importance with any gas appliance and these fires should be installed by a registered gas fitter. In fifty years, however, gas may have almost run out and, therefore, it is a good idea to alternate fuels. Fuel-effect fires are ideal if you do not want the bother of lighting a real fire or cleaning away ash. But, as long as forests are replanted, real wood fires will be part of the future and gas fuel-effect fires will be tomorrow's antiques.

chimneys and can easily ignite if not cleaned. Cleaning the chimney regularly to prevent an unclear passage considerably reduces fuel consumption.

The use of modern fuels and heating appliances is almost certain to cause condensation as the by-product of combustion. The chemical contained in the condensation can cause progressive deterioration of the brickwork if the flue is defective. Defective flues can be dangerous and are a frequent cause of chimney fires. The mortar rendering of a flue deteriorates with age, resulting in cracks in the liner joints that facilitate sparks and smoke penetration to adjoining timbers. If there is any doubt about the condition of the flue, a smoke test, as described on page 114, is a safe precaution and will show up any leaks or blockages. If serious leaks are found the flue should be relined.

Advanced stages of chemical erosion also seriously affect the chimney, and it may have to be taken down and rebuilt. If more than a quarter of the thickness of the brick or stonework has been worn away, the decayed sections should be carefully cut out and replaced with matching materials. If, however, the erosion is mild, restoring the pointing may be the solution. Rake out old mortar and brush away loose dust before applying the new mortar to provide strong adhesion. Surplus mortar should be brushed off to expose a coarse aggregate before it sets.

Chemical erosion on unlined chimneys can, in addition, be recognized by a bend in the stack, vertical splitting, displacement of chimney pots, and obvious staining.

Dampness

The problems of damp penetration not only affects the chimney but can spread to the roof and the whole building, causing major damage. A fireplace that has not been used for some time has not been keeping the chimney dry; damp may well have set in. If the chimney has not been capped to keep out the rain and there has not been enough ventilation, the brickwork may be seriously eroded by damp. If the walls have been saturated by rain, which can happen if they are less than 9 inches (23 cm) in depth, they could be badly decayed. A chimney in this condition will need to be relined, strengthened, or rebuilt. Waterproof flashing, made of suitable sheet metal, must be placed between the base of the chimney and the roof. This, along with suitable protection at the top of the chimney, should prevent damp. Before weatherproof flashing is fitted, it is advisable to put in damp-proof courses under the capping and at the junction of the roof.

Dampness is often caused by unventilated flues in centrally heated houses. If damp has penetrated the interior chimney breast and the problem is mild, the brickwork should be replastered and sealed with aluminum paint. If the damage is extensive the flue must be relined and the wall coated with a bituminous membrane and then replastered. Ventilation must be provided at the top and bottom of the flue to keep dampness at bay.

The Throat

The throat of the fireplace is where the walls of the fireplace gather to meet the flue. It enables the fire to operate effectively by restricting the amount of air flowing from the room up the chimney and preventing heat from being wasted. Metal dampers can also be fitted to the throat to control air flow. Dampers regulate the size of the opening to allow the fire to burn with the minimum amount of air flow. When the fire is not in use the flue can be closed completely. Throat restricters or dampers can be very useful in curing a smoky fireplace. If your fireplace does not possess a throat, prefabricated throats made of iron or fireclay are available.

The Hearth

The purpose of the hearth is to protect the floor from heat, sparks, and falling coal or logs; it should therefore be constructed of a noncombustible material, such as marble, slate, or tiles.

Although the fireplace and chimney may be in poor condition, it is quite possible that the constructional hearth will need little actual restoration unless the foundations have sunk. In this case the whole structure may be in jeopardy and will need rebuilding. Any older hearth may not have an adequate fireproof underlay. If you are unsure about the fire safety element or the structural stability of your hearth, seek professional advice.

Many fireplaces have a more decorative hearth of tiles, brick, or stone laid on top of the constructional hearth, which is usually concrete or another strong noncumbustible material. Additional insulation under the hearth is advisable, particularly where timber joists are present. Concrete, solid bricks, or a metal plate with noncombustible cement underlay is the best insulator. The fire risk is greater where a new floor has been laid over an old one and the hearth is in a sunken position. The hearth must be checked for any cracks or gaps and repaired. It should also be flush with the floor or slightly raised. If the hearth is below the level of the floor, there is always a risk of sparks setting the floor alight.

Ideally, hearths should extend beyond the fireplace opening at least 20 inches (50 cm) and to each side of it by at least 6 inches (15 cm). In the case of hearths to be tiled, very common in late Victorian and Edwardian times, the tiles should be laid on a bed of reinforced concrete, at least 3¼ inches (8.5 cm) thick. Tiles act as a good insulator and need to be about ½ inch (1 cm) thick. Victorian tiles were usually 6 inches (15 cm) square, and the average

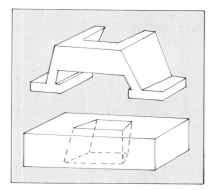

If your fireplace does not have a throat, prefabricated throat units are available in iron or fireclay. These can stand on brick piers and have a removable insert that forms the throat and gives access for filling in behind the fire.

The hearth is a solid slab of concrete, called a constructional hearth, which extends into the room in front of the opening. This is usually covered by a separate slab of tiled concrete, marble, or slate, called the superimposed or decorative hearth.

hearth consisted of about 30 tiles, which were often the only nonferrous element in a fireplace. Decorative tiles, some of which were hand-painted, placed on either side of the fireplace in the cast-iron insert, were typical of the period. Embossed tiles of various sizes became popular during the Edwardian age. Nowadays original Victorian tiles are collector's items and therefore expensive, but as a result of the revival of interest in the period, there is an enormous range of reproduction tiles from which to choose.

Installing a Stove

The easiest and safest way to install a stove is to fit it into an existing fireplace, providing that hearth and recess masonry are in good order. If you do not wish to install your stove in a fireplace recess but want it freestanding, the general safety rules are to leave at least 36 inches (92 cm) between the stove and any combustible material; flues and stovepipes must be insulated where they pass through the walls, ceilings, and roof; combustible walls and floors near the stove must be protected with a noncombustible material. In all cases, follow the manufacturer's directions and conform to local building codes.

Be sure that all stove and flue connections are firm. If they are not, there is the risk of sparks escaping and a poor draft. To test the safety of the flue, once the stove is alight, rest the palm of your hand on it; it should not be so hot that it burns you,

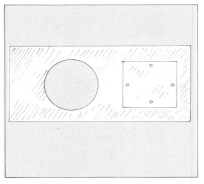

A register plate must be fitted into the chimney to seal it; otherwise the stove will not draw properly. This consists of a steel plate with a hole for the flue and a door through which the chimney can be swept.

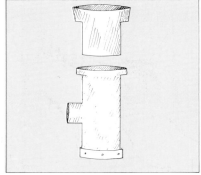

Flue pipes are available in sections and can be extended to any length depending on the position of the chimney.

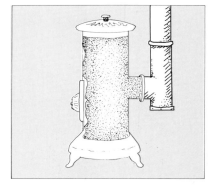

The T-pipe is fitted to the stove using fire cement. This is a form of putty and must be kept in a tightly sealed bag as it hardens very quickly. Once this has set, move the stove into position and fit the extension pipe to the stove and through the hole in the register. Seal both with fire cement. Make sure all connections are firm, otherwise the stove will not draw properly and there will be the risk of sparks escaping.

even at its hottest points, which are at the bends.*

Smoke Problems

Throughout the ages smoky fires have been an unwelcome fact of life. Countless designers and inventors have come up with theories to solve the problem. During the eighteenth and nineteenth centuries the hazards of a smoky chimney reached a drastic peak. Thick, black noxious coal smoke poured into the skies and inevitably into people's rooms. Some developments to cure smoking only polluted the outside atmosphere even more and led to the asphyxiating city fogs. In Leeds, England, it was estimated in 1910 that the waste of fuel amounted to 20 tons of unburned coal discharged into the atmosphere every twelve hours.

With today's stricter regulations and more efficient heating appliances, this is not such a problem, but still chimneys misbehave and blow smoke back into our comfortable rooms. There are many reasons for this, and fortunately there are quite a few remedies.

The fault usually lies in the flue and in rooms where there is insufficient draft to pull the smoke up and out of the chimney. If there is insufficient draft you will find that the smoking stops when you open a door or window. One way to test the draw of the flue is to try the smoke test, as described on page 114. If the flue draws well the smoke should go directly up the chimney, but if it does not the

Downdrafts, caused by nearby hills, adjacent tall buildings, or trees can deflect wind to blow directly down the flue, filling the room with smoke. This problem can be remedied by fitting a cowl.

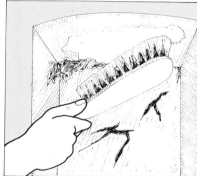

If a fireback is cracked, smoke and heat can penetrate behind the fireplace and eventually weaken the structure of the chimney. To check for cracks, brush with a stiff hand brush to remove soot and loose dirt.

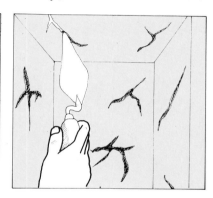

Rake out the cracks with a sharply pointed tool. Clean any loose particles away with a stiff brush, and brush each side of the cracks.

*Important Note: The Environmental Protection Administration has established national standards for all stoves manufactured after July 1, 1989. Non-certified stoves may still be sold until July 1, 1991. In general, certified stoves are safer and more efficient. Check with your dealer and look for the EPA certification label.

smoke will drift back into the room.

One way to help the flue draw better is to reduce the opening of the throat. Adding a means of ventilation, such as a small grill in the hearth or fireplace walls, is another cure.

The size and shape of the fireplace opening also affect smoking. The "Victorian arch" was supposedly designed to alleviate smoking problems. If you suspect that the problem is a result of the opening being too high or wide, place a piece of cardboard across the top and down the sides. Then test the draw of the flue with the smoke test to see if reducing the area helps. Fitting a strip of toughened glass, a canopy, or metal plate could be an easy and cheap permanent solution to the problem.

Alternatively the hearth could be raised, but if you do not wish to alter the look of your fireplace, add a metal register or new liner to modify the flue dimensions – a solution that is probably best left to a professional.

Smoking problems are quite often a sign that the flue needs cleaning or has become blocked. Have the chimney professionally swept and see whether this does the job; if not you may need to consider rebuilding.

If there are too many bends in the flue, the draw may be affected and blockages occur more frequently. The size of shape of the throat, the entrance to the flue, may be incorrect and you may need to alter or replace it. Again you can discover

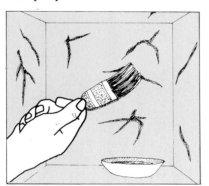

Soak the cracks thoroughly with water to prevent the fireback from absorbing too much water from the filler. Work the water well into the cracks.

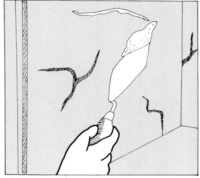

Using a trowel or putty knife, fill the cracks with plastic fireclay before the water has a chance to dry out, pressing the fireclay into the cracks as firmly as possible.

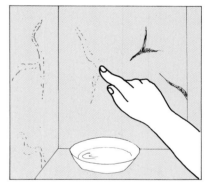

Remove any excess clay with a finger dipped in water, and smooth the surface.

whether it is preventing the flue from drawing properly by restricting the throat with a sheet of cardboard and carrying out the smoke test.

Air leaks due to defective lining also diminish the effect of the draw, and you will need to replace the lining or repair it with a lining compound. Unsuitable chimney pots could cause smoking, but are generally only partly to blame. Before you can isolate the cause of your smoking fire, repair any faulty joints or cracks in the entire chimney and fireplace.

If you suspect that the smoking problem is related to a high-pressure wind outside, it is possible that the chimney needs to be extended or that a cowl should be fitted. Low-pressure winds suck the smoke back into the room and this problem should also be solved by fitting a cowl. Neighboring trees and tall buildings may also interfere with the draw and a chimney cowl will remedy this cause of smoking, too.

Drafts

The image of being snug and cosy by the open fire is synonymous with having defeated nature's bitterly cold winter. To burn well, open fires must have air entering the room. You can avoid cold drafts, but both you and the fire need a steady flow of fresh air to survive. Air starvation can cause smoky chimneys. Old homes allowed a stream of air ventilation through the gap between the bottom of

If the fireback is badly damaged a new one will have to be fitted. Carefully break away the old one with a hammer and chisel and remove all broken pieces.

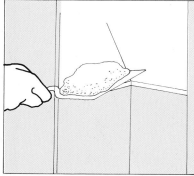

A replacement fireback usually comes in two halves so that it can be fitted and cemented correctly. Fit the lower half into the opening, making sure that it stands squarely and centrally in the opening. Pack a mixture of lime, cement, and sand (1:1:9) into the space behind the fireback.

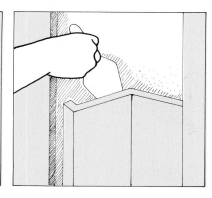

Completely fill the space behind the fireback, pushing the mixture well down with a trowel.

doors and the floor, but today's double glazing and wall-to-wall carpeting may prevent this airflow, resulting in insufficient air in the room to replace that being drawn up the chimney. To remedy this problem, fix floor grills near the hearth in timber floors or, where there are solid floors, remove draft-proof strips from doors or place a grill near the door.

The Fireback

Cracks in a fireback allow smoke and heat to escape from the fireplace. This eventually weakens the structure of the chimney and may also be a fire risk.

If there are major cracks in the fireback a new fireback may need to be fitted. Small cracks can be repaired with fire cement or plastic fireclay. To do this, soak the fireback thoroughly with water to prevent liquid from being drawn out of the cement. Press the mix firmly into the cracks with a trowel, and then wipe off any excess cement with water and allow it to set.

Restoring the Timber Mantel

Clean the timber with a soft brush and warm, soapy water, but do not allow it to become saturated because it may split when the fire quickly dries it out again. This is a particular risk with a softwood, such as pine. Any glue should be removed before polishing or it will show up even more. Use a good quality wax-based furniture polish with a soft cloth.

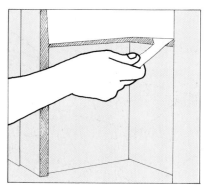

Fit the top section of the fireback into the opening, seating it squarely on the bottom half and levering it into place with a bolster.

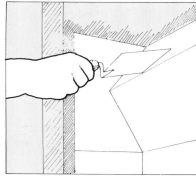

Pack the same weak mixture of lime, cement, and sand into the space behind the top section, and when the cavity is filled to the top, slope a layer of rendering cement to meet the brickwork at the back of the chimney. Wet the joint between the top and bottom sections, fill with fire cement, and smooth with a trowel.

Tiles in front of the fire often craze and crack because of the heat. Carefully chip out the damaged tile, taking care not to damage the edges of the adjoining tiles. Lift out the pieces, making sure that the base is clean and even.

Do not use a silicon polish or it will merely lie on the surface like a sealant. Timber needs to be fed regularly to prevent cracking, and a good polish will seep in and highlight the natural grain.

To repair chipped or damaged timber, try using a commercial beeswax. Melt the wax and add vegetable dye to the color required to match the timber. Once the wax is set the damaged area can be filled by remelting it onto the timber. When it has cooled and set, shave any excess wax off for a smooth finish. Lightly sandpaper the repair so that it blends with the existing timber. Then wipe the surface clean and polish. Holes made by woodworm infestation can be filled in this way, too, but first you need to apply an insecticide.

Place a new tile in the space, and make sure that it lies flat and flush with the adjoining tiles.

Remove the tile, and apply the appropriate adhesive to the tile and to the hearth, taking care not to spread it on the sides of the adjacent tiles.

Place the tile carefully into the space, and press firmly into position with the fingers. Remove any excess adhesive with a damp cloth, and when set, fill with heat-resistant grout. To give a neat finish, trace around the tile with a round-ended stick.

If your mantelpiece is painted timber and you want to remove the paint, there are various factors to consider before embarking. Many fireplaces were designed to be painted to echo the color schemes of the paneled room and cornices. This is particularly applicable to those of the 1760–1800 period and, as a result, an inferior wood was often used.

If you plan to strip other furnishings, doors, and floors, you should be aware that you may be left with a mixture of different timbers with considerable variance in grain and color. Mantelpieces were sometimes painted to cover stains or cracks, and it is a good idea to strip one side of the leg first to get an idea of what lies beneath the paint. This will enable you to find out whether it is advisable to expose the wood at all.

If you decide to strip the paint you may need to remove the surround from the wall and must consider whether you need specialist help. By removing the surround, either in sections or as a whole, it will be easier to strip the paint. Once dismantled it can be placed in a caustic bath. This will take approximately one to two days and must be checked at regular intervals. However, some detail may be lost on the carved areas. If the carving on the fireplace is gesso, do not used the caustic bath method. Carvings that are heavily clogged with paint are always difficult to clean. The alternative to using a caustic bath is to use a proprietary paint stripper. This can be applied when the mantelpiece

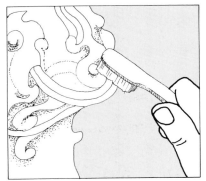

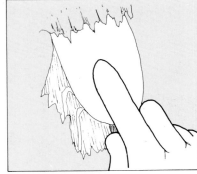

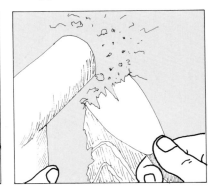

Clean the timber with a soft brush and warm, soapy water, but do not allow it to become saturated because there is the danger of the wood splitting when the fire is relit. Clean dirty carvings with an old toothbrush.

If you wish to remove old paint finishes, apply a proprietary paint stripper with an old paintbrush, following the manufacturer's instructions carefully. When the paint surface bubbles, remove it with a paint scraper. Make sure that the room is well ventilated, as the fumes are very strong. Wear gloves as the liquid can burn the skin. If the carved areas are made of gesso take special care as the caustic liquid will cause the gesso to dissolve if left in contact for more than a few minutes.

If the surround does not have complicated carvings, an alternative method is to use an electric hot air stripper. Propane torches are not recommended, as it is easy to scorch the underlying wood. Once the paint finish has been removed, rub down the wood with fine sandpaper or steel wool. The surface is now ready for repolishing or painting.

is still attached to the wall. Do it by hand and as gently as possible.

Restoring the Marble Mantelpiece

If your house has an original marble fireplace in need of restoration, the following hints may solve your problems. Buying an unrestored, antique marble fireplace to install in your house can be a gamble. It may be filthy and even deliberately covered with dirt or paint to hide stains or cracks. Smoke stains can ruin the look of marble and, in some cases, are impossible to remove. Oil stains cannot be removed either. It is not worth buying an antique marble fireplace unless you think you will be able to remove the stains or, alternatively, if you are quite content to live with them.

Marble is 99 percent calcium carbonate and very porous. Stains are absorbed deep into the pores, so when cleaning marble do not use acids, dyes, or alcohol as these, too, soak in and stain, eventually causing the marble to rot. Smoke stains are the most common problem and can leave the marble badly discolored. Pot plants and glasses also cause staining. Scrubbing does very little, although sometimes the shallow surface stains can be removed with an abrasive cleaner. If you do use an abrasive cleaner, the smooth marble surface can be restored by buffing and polishing. Never use stiff-bristled brushes as they can scratch the surface.

The only effective way to remove stains is to apply

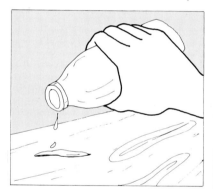

To remove French polish apply a drop of methylated spirits (denatured alcohol).

Rub the finish with a small piece of fine steel wool until a "gravy" appears. Remember to work along the grain, not across it or in circles, as this leaves scratches that are difficult to remove. Remove the dissolved polish with paper towels or old rags.

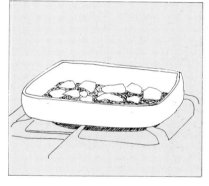

It is possible to repair chips or cracks in the surround with melted beeswax, which can be colored to match the wood with vegetable dyes. Break the beeswax into small pieces and melt them slowly on a burner.

a mud poultice that can draw out the embedded stains. Commercial poultices have a drawing agent made up of paint whiting and hydrogen peroxide. Be generous when applying the poultice, and cover the area with a large sheet of plastic, to keep the poultice relatively moist. Secure the plastic sheet by taping down the edges. This process can take between two to three days to complete. Wash down the surface and inspect. It may be necessary to give the marble a second application, depending on the severity of the stain.

Once the staining is removed, polish the marble with a white, hard polish for a highly polished finish or a softer polish for a mat finish. Rub polish hard into the marble using a soft white cloth.

Restoring a marble fireplace is time consuming and tedious. Installing a marble fireplace is also a heavy, dirty, and skilled job, so consider the help of a specialist.

Some specialists carry out the restoration on site. You can remove paint yourself, if you wish, by using a proprietary paint stripper, but wear rubber gloves to protect skin and clothing. If a lead-based paint has been used, it is a worse problem to remove and may have damaged the marble. Work with the paint stripper on a few square inches at a time. Remove excess stripper with acetone on small swabs of cotton wool. Repeat until paint disappears. Be careful if using a paint scraper, because marble is easily scratched.

Once it has melted, remove it from the heat and gradually add small quantities of powdered vegetable dye to the wax, taking care not to overcolor it. Thoroughly mix the dye each time it is added to the wax, constantly checking for color.

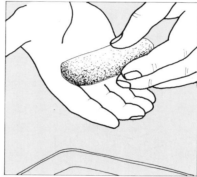

When a suitable color has been achieved, leave the wax to set. Then prise it out of the tin in pieces and roll the wax into a sausage shape between both hands. Check once again for color.

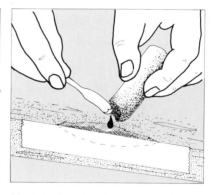

Heat the handle of a spoon and, holding the roll of wax over the damaged area, melt the wax into the cracks. In the case of a chip, stick a piece of adhesive tape against the damaged section. Overfill the cracks to allow for shrinkage as it cools.

Cracks in marble are quite a common problem. If your fireplace is badly damaged you may need to take it down in pieces and reassemble from scratch. You may also need some extra pieces of marble to mend larger cracks or breaks.

Refitting smaller pieces of marble can be done with an epoxy resin adhesive. First clean away any dirt from the two surfaces to be glued together. Press the broken piece into place, and immediately remove any surplus adhesive with a knife. Secure the mend with a piece of tape, until set. If marble is only chipped you can make up a paste to fill the chips. This may not be easy and is often best left to the specialist restorer. Before you embark upon expensive and laborious work, consider the degree of restoration you want. You may not necessarily want your mantelpiece to look brand new. Carrara marble is easier to fill because of its grayish look, but with white marble it is virtually impossible to disguise the mends and hardeners can change color once they are set. However, in many cases it can be quite successful and it would be worth trying on a less noticeable section first. Mix a colored marble glue or an epoxy resin adhesive mixed with vegetable dye to match the surrounding marble. Once it has been applied, leave it to set and then rub down with a fine wet and dry sandpaper, until the mended section blends with the surface. Pumice can be used to smooth the area.

Complete the procedure by polishing the surface.

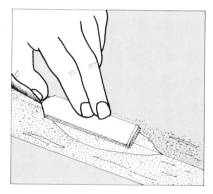

When the wax has cooled and set, hold a wide chisel flat against the surface and shave the wax filling to a smooth and even finish.

Sand the area gently with very fine sandpaper until the edges of the wax blend into the woodwork. Then polish the repaired area to match the timber. This also seals the wax filling. Other good fillers include stick shellac and plasticized wood.

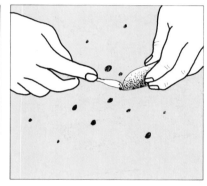

This method can also be used to fill holes made by woodworm, provided that the area has first been treated with a proprietary insecticide.

Stone

Stone mantelpieces were generally meant to be painted. However, if you wish to remove the paint, follow the same guidelines as for marble. When cleaning stone do not use acid. Mix a strong solution of water and mild detergent and then apply it with a stiff, but not harsh, bristle brush. Follow with warm water to wash the surface clean.

To replace a loose piece of stone, remove any loose debris or cement and clean the area. Soak both surfaces and then refit the stone with a mortar mix of sand and cement in a ratio of 3:1. Apply a generous amount of mortar, using a straightedge or level to ensure that the stone is flush with the existing stonework. When it is almost dry, clean off the excess mortar with a soft brush followed by a wet sponge to prevent any mortar from staining the surface.

Brick

Bricks surrounding a fireplace can become damaged from extremes of temperature and from coal fumes. Fumes cause the mortar to deteriorate, and if bricks are loose you must refit them. Clean away the mortar from the surface of the adjoining bricks. Wet the brick thoroughly. Apply a ½ inch (1.2 cm) layer of mortar mix (3:1 mix of sand and cement) to the back and sides of the brick. Position it, and tap gently into place. To repoint, prepare a mortar mixture of 1 part sulfate-resistant cement, 3

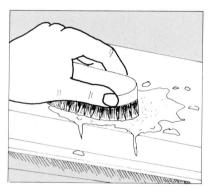

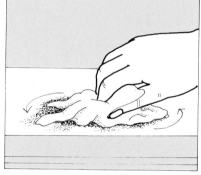

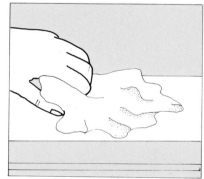

Wash the marble with the following solution: dissolve a cup of pure soap powder (not detergent) in a gallon of water to which a few drops of ammonia have been added. Work across the surface with a pure bristle brush, allowing a constant stream of water to run over the area, rinsing and wiping with clean *white* rags as you go. Do not use colored rags as the dye may come out.

Examine the mantelpiece for chips and stains. If the damage is not serious polishing should restore the surface. Rub pumice or powdered chalk into the stained area using a circular motion. Rinse with clean water and dry with a clean white cloth when the surface feels smooth and the stain has disappeared. If the stains are more serious it is possible to remove them with a poultice, but this is an extremely difficult operation and is best left to the specialist.

When the mantelpiece has been cleaned and any surface stains removed, it can be polished. It is not wise to use a furniture wax as this might stain the marble. However, it is possible to obtain a polish specifically for marble.

parts lime, and 10–12 parts clean heat-resistant sand. Scrape the old mortar out of the joints and brush away loose dust. Press the mortar firmly into the joints, either flush with the bricks or recessed. Clean away excess mortar with a soft brush dampened with water. Do not use soapy water on brick.

Stains on bricks can be removed with a solution of trisodium phosphate (TSP). Mix half a cup of TSP with a gallon of water. After scrubbing thoroughly wash with cold water.

Iron and Steel

Restoring cast iron is dealt with under Restoring a Stove on page 149. It is difficult to repair a cast-iron surround or grate as most professional iron founders may only be able to supply you with a missing piece if it is worthwhile for them to produce hundreds from the same mold. However, it is worth trying a small iron founder who specializes in decorative domestic ironwork. They may be able to recast pieces, such as panels, doors, and other missing or damaged parts to the original design. If possible, take along the existing piece, otherwise make an accurate drawing. An alternative is to use stainless steel.

Paint can be removed from ironwork with a commercial chemical stripper. Once stripped, use a wire brush to remove any rust. If you are repainting use a coat of rust resistant primer prior to the final

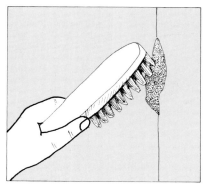

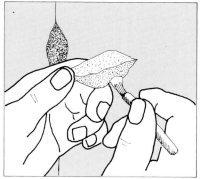

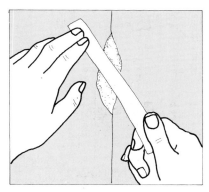

If a piece of marble breaks, it can be stuck back in position with an epoxy resin adhesive. This is a two-part adhesive, and for best results you must follow the manufacturer's instructions carefully. Clean the two surfaces with a stiff brush and rub them with glass-paper.

Mix the two parts of the adhesive together on an old plate or something similar, and using an old paintbrush, apply an even film of the mixture to both surfaces. (Once the two parts of the adhesive have been mixed together they must be used within four hours.)

Press the broken piece into place and secure the mend with a piece of tape until set. Immediately remove any surplus adhesive from the surface with a knife.

coat of paint, to prevent further rusting. Never use ordinary paint on fireplace equipment. There are paints especially for the purpose that can be obtained from most good hardware or paint stores. If you do not wish to paint the ironwork you can give it a good finish with wax polish or blacking, which can be polished to give a burnished steel effect. Areas of the fireplace, such as grates and baskets, that may be prone to rusting due to the cold air or rain coming down the chimney, should be protected with an iron paste or stove black. Another problem is the accumulation of soot and ash. To remove this, scour regularly with a wire brush and either leave the natural finish or apply stove black. This can be polished to give a burnished steel effect.

Steel grates have a finer surface. Strong rust removers should not be used. Clean the surface with a fine steel wool and warm soapy water; do not use a sharp tool or wire brush. Then dry and polish the grate with a soft cloth and mild metal polish.

Fire trims around the opening, made of metal and often enameled, can become burned and stained from the fire. These need to be cleaned regularly. Dirt that is difficult to remove may require the aid of a commercial cleaning pad.

Brass and Ormolu

There are no magical ways to restore brass fittings. You can use a special compound soap for cleaning (a different variety from the one used on

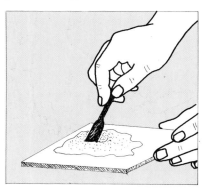

If there are any chips or deep scratches, they can be filled with an epoxy resin adhesive to which a vegetable dye of a matching color has been added. Mix the adhesive on a flat surface and gradually add vegetable dye until the correct color has been obtained.

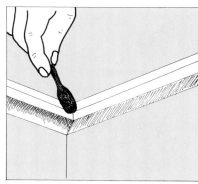

Use a glue spreader to fill the chip with the adhesive, carefully following the contours of the marble. Leave it to set.

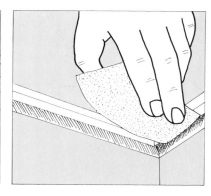

Once it has set, using a fine wet and dry sandpaper rub down the adhesive to shape until it blends in with the surface. Wash the marble with a sponge and clean water to ensure that all dust from the adhesive has been removed. Polish with pumice or powdered chalk as described on page 146.

steel). Clean brass gently and then, if you have access to it, a machine with a mop wheel is ideal for smoothing any rough metal and polish. Otherwise use a good quality mild polish, which will prevent a certain amount of tarnishing. It is generally not a good idea to use lacquer on fireplace equipment. If the brass fitting is removable and not too big, it can be boiled for several hours in a solution of water, white vinegar (1 cup), and salt (1 rounded tablespoonful). This method is particularly successful for badly corroded brass.

Ormolu is cast brass with a gold leaf surface. Do not scrub it with an abrasive or you will remove the gold. The brass underneath may appear shiny but will later turn green. Use a mild soapy water to which a little household ammonia has been added and a pure bristle brush. Do not use a nylon brush as it is too scratchy. Take great care and treat it very gently as the gold surface is only a very thin layer and can easily be destroyed. Frequent polishing is not advisable.

Restoring a Stove

If you are buying an old cast-iron or sheet-metal stove, or if your house has one that has not been used for years, first check for rust, cracks, and missing pieces. Make sure that the body is sound, inside and out, and check the floor and sides of the firebox as these are most likely to be burned out or cracked.

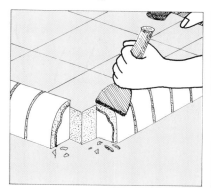

Smoke fumes cause mortar to decay; eventually this results in bricks coming loose, in which case you will need to replace them. First clean away old mortar around the loose brick, using a hammer and bricklayer's chisel. Remove the loose brick.

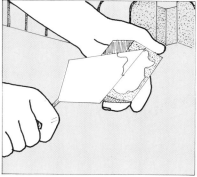

Thoroughly wet the brick you are refitting and apply a ½ inch (1.2 cm) layer of mortar mix (3:1 mix of sand and cement) to the back and sides of the brick.

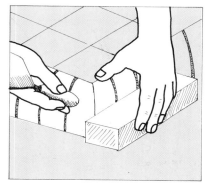

Push the brick back into its gap, carefully and gently tapping it into place with the end of a trowel handle. You can also use a straight piece of wood to line up the brick evenly with existing brickwork.

With an old sheet-metal stove it may be necessary to replace the soft inner lining. It is also possible to patch holes, but it is not worth the time and effort if the stove requires extensive patching. To patch a hole use nickel welding rods and patching metal capable of withstanding a temperature of at least 1000°F. Professional equipment and assistance is recommended; patches put on by household welding torches can come unstuck on a hot stove.

A cast-iron stove can have its interior mended by fitting a new sheet-metal liner. It is a good idea to put a 2 inch (5 cm) layer of sand on the floor of the stove, particularly if there is no grate, to prevent future burning out. The inside grate is often burned out as a result of the stove being overfired and allowed to burn white-hot. Overfiring also causes the grate to buckle or crack. There is a good chance that the grate can simply be replaced. Take the old one along to a salvage yard, a specialist supplier, a building supply store, or an iron monger. If the grate cannot be replaced, add a layer of sand or let a layer of ash build up to protect the bottom of the stove. Another solution is to adapt andirons or use bricks to support the burning wood.

If the cast iron is broken it cannot be satisfactorily rebonded to hold a fire. Glue and welding bonds expand with the heat at different rates to the iron and are therefore only a temporary solution. You really need to replace the entire casing. A foundry may be able to make a special part, but it will be

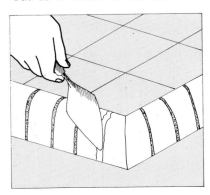

Finally use the tip of the trowel to remove excess mortar to a depth of ½ inch (13 mm). Then repoint the brickwork.

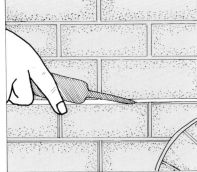

If you are simply repointing brickwork, use the tang end of a file to scrape the old mortar out of the joints to a depth of about ½ inch (13 mm). Brush off loose dust and use a hand brush to soak the brickwork thoroughly with water.

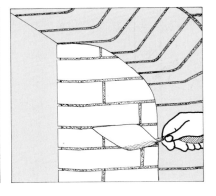

Prepare a mortar mix (1 part sulfate-resistant cement, 3 parts lime, 10–12 parts clean sand). Pile some mortar mix onto a hawk, and press the mortar firmly into the joints with a trowel. Begin with the vertical joints and then repoint the horizontals. The mortar should lie flush with the surface of the adjacent brickwork.

expensive. Remember when examining an old stove that a new coat of paint could be hiding rust or puttied holes. Give it a good "tapping" over to be sure of its worth.

The most commonly missing pieces on an old stove are nuts, bolts, rods, handles, glass windows, metal trims, and sliding draft controls. If a leg is missing a professional welder could make another from angle iron.

Thin cracks of no more than ⅛ inch (3 mm) between seams can be filled with furnace cement. Open seams and warped plates are usually caused by overfiring, particularly from coal fires. This problem may be overcome by installing a fireback or cast-iron liner. When you fire up the stove, treat it gently and do not allow it to get too hot. If the glass window in an airtight or combustion stove is broken, it must be replaced for the stove to operate efficiently; the replacement glass must be able to stand intense heat. It should be easy to restore if the stove is a common brand just by giving the name and model number to the manufacturer.

The standard black cast-iron stove should only need the occasional good polish. If the stove is not being used, it is recommended that it be protected with a special black paint.

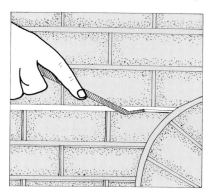

A standard method of giving a clean finish to the pointing is to create recessed joints. Use a trowel to scrape away ½ inch (13 mm) of the new mortar evenly along the joint. (Alternatively, mortar can be left flush with the brickwork.).

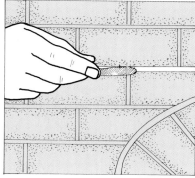

To create a smooth finish to the recessed joints, gently draw a piece of wood along the joint until it is smooth.

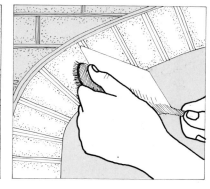

Clean the mortar from the edges of the bricks with a soft brush, dampened with water. To protect the newly repointed joints while you are dong this, hold the trowel over them so that you can brush mortar from the surrounding area. Do not use soapy water on brickwork.

Ormolu is a difficult material to clean. Any abrasive action can result in the complete removal of the gold leaf layer that coats the cast brass. (Although the brass underneath may appear shiny, it tarnishes rapidly.) To clean ormolu use a mild soapy water to which a little household ammonia has been added. Apply the solution carefully using a soft, pure bristle brush. Never use nylon brushes, as this scratches the surface.

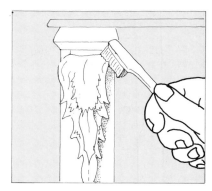

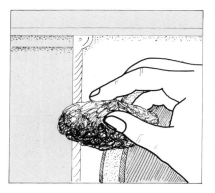

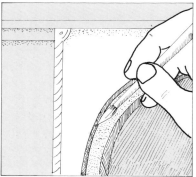

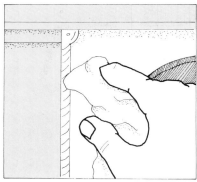

First remove any loose deposits of dirt and rust by scrubbing flat surfaces with fine steel wool pads or silicone carbide abrasive paper. For crevices use a wire brush. Soot and ash should also be removed regularly with a wire brush. (A phosphoric rust remover can be used as well; you should follow the manufacturer's instructions carefully.) For steel grates strong rust removers should be avoided. Instead fine steel wool and warm soapy water can be used.

If the iron is to be painted or repainted, apply a coat of red oxide paint prior to painting. This prevents further rusting. Never use ordinary paint on fireplace equipment. You can buy special paints from hardware and paint stores.

If you do not intend to paint the iron you can finish by polishing the surface with a little silicone furniture wax or stove black. By polishing the stove black you can achieve a burnished steel effect. To keep the cast iron in good condition this should be done fairly regularly. Iron paste or stove black is best used on grates and firebacks, which are most prone to rusting. Steel can be polished with a soft cloth and mild metal polish.

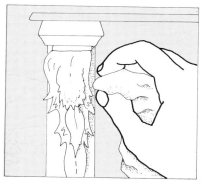

Dry the surface with a clean, dry cloth. Do not polish too often, as you may damage the surface.

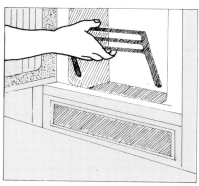

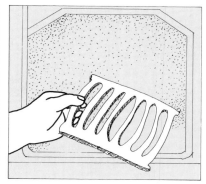

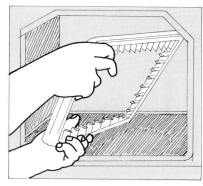

When you renovate a stove that has buckled or cracked fire bars and grating, it is important to dismantle the components in the correct order. It is worth making a note of the order in which you remove parts so that you can reassemble the stove! Remove the ashtray and front fire bars, noting any identification numbers that will be essential when purchasing identical components from a manufacturer or antique stove dealer.

Then lift out the grating. A building supply store should be able to provide an identical one if it has no identification number. Remove the front firebrick, side firebricks, and fire base, again noting any identification numbers.

Replace the new base in the stove so that its pin fits easily into the shaker hole at the back. Replace the other components in the correct order.

MANUFACTURERS & SUPPLIERS

Acquisitions Fireplaces, Ltd.
269 Camden High Street
London NW1 7BX, England

Aga Rayburn
P.O. Box 30
Ketley
Telford
Shropshire TF1 4DD, England

American Energy Systems R.D.N.
50 Academy Lane
Hutchinson, MN 55350

Antique Market
Highway 70
McMinnville, TN 37110

Antiques Ltd.
1517 Merchandise Mart
Chicago, IL 60654

Architectural Antiques Exchange
709-15 N. Second Street
Philadelphia, PA 19123

Architectural Antiques & Reproductions
(Levy Gascolier Antiques)
1151 K Street NW
Washington, DC 20005

Beckwood Industries, Inc.
889 Horan Drive
Fenton, MO 63026

Bennington Bronze
P.O. 183
Woodbury, CT 06798

Cantabrian Antiques
Park Street
Lynton
Devon, England

The Cast Iron Fireplace Co., Ltd.
103 East Hill
Wandsworth
London SW18, England

Clovis Fires
Branbridges Road
East Peckham
Kent TN12 5HH, England

Country Flame
P.O. Box 151
Mt. Vernon, MO 65712

Custom Firescreen, Inc.
108 Jefferson Avenue
Des Moines, IA 50314

Dagan Industries, Inc.
15540 Roxford Street
Sylmar, CA 91342

Daris & Warshaw, Inc.
1033 Third Avenue
New York, NY 10021

Designer Resource
5160 Melrose Avenue
Los Angeles, CA 90038

Dovre Castings
Unit 81
Castle Vale Industrial Estate
Minworth
Sutton Coldfield B76 8AL, England

Entasis
5301 Westbard Circle #119
Bethesda, MD 20816

Eric Anthony Reproductions
8730 Santa Monica Boulevard
P.O. Box 69686
Los Angeles, CA 90069

Fiori Designs
25 Amity Street
Little Falls, NJ 07424

Focal Point, Inc.
2004 Marietta Road NW
Atlanta, GA 30318

Fondis Corporation
P.O. Box 6444
Edison, NJ 08818

Franco-Belge
Unit 91
Castle Vale Industrial Estate
Minworth
Sutton Coldfield B76 8AL, England

Freestanding Fireplaces, Inc.
Route 52
Jeffersonville, NY 12748

Gasline Corporation
1605 West Railroad Street
Corona, CA 91720

Heat-N-Glo Corporation
6665 West Highway 13 Drive
Savage, MN 55378

Heatilator, Inc.
1915 West Saunders Road
Mt. Pleasant, IA 52641

Holden Heat plc
Court Farm Trading Estate
Bishops Frome
Worcs WR6 5AY, England

Home & Hearth, Inc.
1550 Simpson Way
Escondido, CA 92025

Hunter Enterprises Orillia, Ltd.
P.O. Box 400
Orillia, Ont. L3V 614, Canada

Ideal Fireplaces, Ltd.
300 Upper Richmond Road West
East Sheen
London SW14 7JG, England

Jotul USA, Inc.
400 Riverside Street
P.O. Box 1157
Portland, ME 04104

K & W Fireplace & BBQ
23107 Temescal Canyon Road
Corona, CA 91719

Kingsworthy Foundry
Winchester
Hampshire, England

LaBelle Cheminée, Ltd.
85 Wigmore Street
London W1H 9FA, England

Lakewood Stove Co., Ltd.
P.O. Box 489
Bobcargeon, Ont. KOM 1AO, Canada

Locke Home Productions, Inc.
4200 St. Clair Avenue
Washington Park, IL 62204

The Majestic Company
EBP Holdings, Inc.
1000 East Market Street
Huntington, IN 46750

Majestic Fireplaces, Inc.
Jealen Distributors
P.O. Box 119
Staten Island, NY 10306

Malm Fireplaces, Inc.
368 Yolanda Avenue
Santa Rosa, CA 95404

Marble Hill
72 Richmond Road
Twickenham
Middlesex, England

Marco Manufacturing, Inc.
2520 Industry Way
Lynwood, CA 90262

Martin Industries
P.O. Box 128
Florence, AL 35631

Mendota Forge Corporation
1890 Wooddale Drive
P.O. Box 25007
St. Paul, MN 55125

Napoleon Fireplaces
Wolf Steel Ltd.
Rural Route #1
Highway 11 and 93
Barrie, Ont. L4M 4Y8, Canada

New Buck Stove Corporation
1265 Bakersville Highway
Spruce Pine, NC 28777

The North Carolina Granite Corp.
Quarry Road
P.O. Box 151
Mount Airy, NC 27030

Nostalgia, Inc.
307 Stiles Avenue
Savannah, GA 31401

Okell's Fireplace
134 Pacific Coast Highway
Hermosa Beach, CA 90254

Old World Moulding & Finishing Co., Inc.
115 Allen Boulevard
Farmingdale, NY 11735

Orion
1628 Oak Lawn
Dallas, TX 75207

Orrville Products, Inc.
375 East Orr Street
P.O. Box 902
Orrville, OH 44667

Osburn Manufacturing, Inc.
555 Ardersier Road
Victoria, BC V8Z 1C8, Canada

Petit Roque
5 New Road
Croxley Green
Rickmansworth, England

Piazetta
John Wood Marketing
7 Braithwaite Way
Frome
Somerset BA11 2XE, England

Rasmussen Iron Works, Inc.
12028 East Philadelphia Street
Whittier, CA 90601

Real Flame
80 Kings Road
London SW15, England

Robin Gage
50 Pimlico Road
London SW1 W8LP, England

Rustic Crafts Co., Inc.
P.O. Box 1085
Scranton, PA 18501

The Readybuilt Products Co.
1701 McHenry Street
P.O. Box 4425
Baltimore, MD 21223

Richard le Droft Fireplaces
c/o Adames Company
1003 Fourth Street
Dubuque, IA 52001

Ruega Fireplaces, Inc.
976 Route 22E
Bridgewater, NJ 08807

Schaeter Company
601 North Long Street
Salisbury, NC 28145

Security Chimneys, Ltd.
2125 Monterey
Laval, Que H7L 3TG, Canada

Selkirk Metalbestos
P.O. Box 372
Nampa, ID 83653

The Strassel Company
1000 Hamilton Avenue
Louisville, KY 40204

Strax Distribution Ltd.
41B Brecknock Road
London N7 0BT, England

Stuart Interiors
Barrington Court
Barrington
Ilminster
Somerset TA19 0NQ, England

Sunset Fireplace Fixtures, Inc.
14940 East Don Julian Road
Industry, CA 91744

Tempte Products
P.O. Box 1184
Nashville, TN 37202

TESS, Inc.
Rural Route 1, Box 3
Beanville Road
Randolph, VT 05060

Thermocet UK
Real Fire Heating Centre
Telford Way
Kettering NN16 8UN, England

Valor, Inc.
699 West Main Street
P.O. Box 1629
Hendersonville, TN 37077

Vermont Castings
4783 Prince Street
Randolph, VT 05060

W. G. Builders, Inc.
Route 2, Box 48
Angier, NC 27501

Wilkening Fireplace Company
H.C.R. 73
Box 625
Walker, MN 56484

Wyndham Fireplace Company, Inc.
2 Parkway & Route 17 South
Upper Saddle River, NJ 07458

Ye Olde Mantel Shoppe
3800 NE Second Avenue
Miami, FL 33137

GLOSSARY

Aga A closed iron range designed on the heat storage principle by Dr. Gustav Dalen in 1924. The stoves can be fueled by coke, oil, or gas.

Air brick Brick that is hollow or perforated.

Anthemion An ancient Greek design based loosely on the honeysuckle, with shapes or lines radiating upward from a base point.

Art deco An art movement of the Jazz Age (1920s and 1930s) that had its greatest impact on the design of jewelry, clothing, and interior decoration. The style is notable for its bold contrasts, sleek lines, and flat, angular shapes. Important examples include New York's Chrysler building and the paintings of Erté.

Art nouveau An art movement of the 1890s and early 1900s that utilized undulating lines and stylized plant motifs. Notable examples include the glass designs of Louis Comfort Tiffany, the curved architecture of Antonio Guardí, and the furniture of Hector Guimard, who also designed the entrances of the Paris Metro.

Baroque An art movement of the seventeenth century characterized by its grandeur and monumentality. Movement, as in Bernini's designs for the Vatican, and dramatic lighting, as in the paintings of Caravaggio and Rembrandt, were also used to achieve impressive effects.

Bas relief A low relief in which the sculpted figures protrude only slightly above the flat planes of the background.

Bossi work A technique of carving white marble and then refilling it with colored marble.

Carrara marble A highly regarded white Italian marble.

Chinoiserie Chinese-style designs and decorations executed by Western craftsmen.

Classical style A style in art and architecture that drew its inspiration from the beautifully balanced and perfectly proportioned structures of ancient Greece and Rome.

Cloam oven An oven built into the side of an inglenook fireplace.

Corbel A weight-bearing projection from a wall.

Echinus A Greek design consisting of oval forms alternating with thin vertical lines. The design was often used in moldings and around capitals of columns.

Eclecticism An approach, which, in the decorative arts, involves the mingling of objects or styles from various schools or periods to produce a strikingly varied overall effect.

Edwardian An ornate, post-Victorian style of decorative art that prevailed during the reign of Edward VII (1901 to 1910).

Elizabethan An ornamented and somewhat haphazard approach to architecture and decoration that characterized the reign of Elizabeth I (1558 to 1603).

Empire A period in French decorative arts that began during Napoleon's reign as emperor and remained popular until the 1830s. Intended to convey a sense of grandeur, it made much use of *Egyptian* motifs (associated with the French conquest of Egypt).

Fender Low metal guard rails or mesh screening designed to confine ashes and burning coals to the hearth.

Fireback A decorative metal shield designed to protect the back wall of a fireplace.

Firebasket An elevated basket made of metal bars originally designed to contain burning coals.

Firedogs Double andirons.

Fire Screen A decorative screen designed to keep sparks from flying into the room.

Fluting A series of shallow, parallel grooves cut into a flat or rounded surface.

Georgian style A return to classical principles in art and architecture that characterized much of the reigns of George I, II, and III (roughly coinciding with the eighteenth century).

Gesso Molded plaster, which produces the effect of carving.

Gothick style An eighteenth century fantasy style of ornamentation based on the elaboration of Gothic designs.

Gothic style A style of Western European architecture that evolved between the twelfth and the early sixteenth centuries. It is exemplified by the soaring cathedrals of France, England, and Germany (e.g., Chartres, Salisbury, Cologne) in which high vaulted ceilings and pointed arches with huge stained glass windows are made possible by supports (flying buttresses) located on the outside of the structure.

Hob A support for a kettle built into the back or side of a fireplace.

Inglenook A large recess in the wall surrounding a fireplace.

Jacobean The style of art and architecture that characterized the reign of James I (1602 to 1625).

Key pattern The Greek key (or fret) is the most famous of Greek designs. It consists of vertical lines with horizontals set at right angles, forming a repetitive border ornamentation.

Neoclassical style A revival of classical principles in art and architecture.

Palladian A *neoclassical* style in architecture based on the principles set forth by the Italian architect, Palladio (1508 to 1580).

Picture rail A molding placed high on a wall from which pictures may be hung.

Queen Anne style A transitional style of the early eighteenth century marked by strong Dutch influence.

Regency The decorative and architectural style of the period when George IV served as regent and reigned as king (1820 to 1830). Although there were extravagances based on oriental motifs, the predominant trend was neoclassicism of extreme elegance and gracefulness.

Rococo An elegant and aristocratic artistic style of the eighteenth century. In both the fine and decorative arts, it is marked by curved, entwined ornamentation based on sea shells, leaves, and flowers, and by shimmering surface patterns. In painting it is exemplified by Watteau and Fragonard in France, and by Tiepolo in Italy.

Roundel A round panel or window.

Scagiola An artificially formed marble made of powdered marble, lime, gypsum, and sometimes plaster. During the eighteenth century it became quite fashionable in its own right.

Surround The area around an architectural detail.

Victorian An eclectic style of architecture and decoration that prevailed during the reign of Victoria (1837 to 1901). It is characterized by a Gothic revival and by advanced technological styles (the iron and glass Crystal Palace is an example of the latter). Interiors were frequently overstuffed and overdecorated.

INDEX

INDEX

Picture Credits

Acquisition Fireplaces Ltd. Contents page, 6, 7, 34 (top), 35, 40, 42 (top), 49 (bottom), 75, 91 (left), 92, 97 (right), 126, 127. Aga Rayburn 63, 64, 65 (top), 67 (bottom), 71, 72 (top), 90, 102. Barkers Creek, Castlemaine, Victoria, Australia 68, 87. Cantabrian Antiques 89 (right). The Cast Iron Fireplace Co. Ltd. Half-title page, 31, 48 (top), 77, 82 (bottom), 93. Clovis Fires Ltd. 15. Como House, Melbourne, Victoria, Australia 32 (bottom), 37 (left), 61, 76, 83, 88, 110. Dovre Casting Ltd. 52. Fired Earth 78. Franco-Belge 70. Holden Heat plc 59. Ideal Fireplaces 34 (bottom), 54, 57, 73, 91 (right), 94, 95, 97 (left), 104, 105, 106, 107. Kingsworth Foundry 105. LaBelle Cheminée 50, 89 (left). Magnafire 60. Marble Hill Fireplaces Ltd. 36, 42 (bottom), 99. Montsalvat, Melbourne, Victoria, Australia 9, 12, 13, 51 (left), 56, 63, 79, 85, 86, 103. National Trust 14, 22, 23, 24, 25, 26, 27, 28, 29, 44, 45, 46, 66, 67 (top). Piazetta 65 (bottom). Petite Roque 8, 84. Portable Iron House, Melbourne, Victoria, Australia 51 (right), 113. Real Flame Log Fires 39, 41. Robin Gage 81. Strax Title page, 10. Stuart Interiors 18, 19, 21 (top). Thermocet UK 53, 55, 69, 72 (bottom), 82 (top), 96. Tony Cook, Castlemaine, Victoria, Australia 80.

Acknowledgements

The photographs on the following pages were taken by Kirsty McClaren: 9, 11, 12, 13, 14, 16, 17, 20, 21 Bottom, 22, 23, 24, 25, 26, 27, 28, 29, 30, 31, 32, 33, 37, 38, 43, 44, 45, 46, 47, 49, 51, 55, 61, 63, 66, 68, 74, 76, 79, 80, 83, 85, 86, 87, 88, 103, 113, 114, 116, 117, 118, 119, 120, 121, 122, 123, 124, 125, 128.